Secrets from an Italian Kitchen

Secrets from an
ITALIAN
KITCHEN

Anna Venturi

PAVILION

Acknowledgements

This book has been made possible thanks to the support of my husband Bill and of my daughters, Letizia and Ilaria, who will carry on our family tradition of Italian cooking and way of life. I also want to thank Elena, Trish, Sally and Suzanne for their invaluable help and friendship.

First published in Great Britain in 2000 by Pavilion Books

This edition published in Great Britain in 2009 by Pavilion Books An imprint of Anova Books Ltd 10 Southcombe Street London W14 0RA

Text © Anna Venturi Photography © Ian Wallace Design and layout © Pavilion Books

A CIP catalogue record for this book is available from the British Library.

ISBN 9781862058606 Set in Swiss 721 light and Palatino Printed and bound by L.E.G.O. SpA, Italy

10 9 8 7 6 5 4 3

This book can be ordered direct from the publisher. Please contact the Marketing Department. But try your bookshop first.

www.anovabooks.com

Contents

Introduction

For many years I have been sharing my secrets of how to cook delicious Italian food with my pupils. When I first started teaching Italian cookery in my family kitchen, I quickly saw how these secrets, never found in cookbooks, made all the difference between success and failure. 'Anna!' my pupils would say, 'What a difference!' The tips have learned from my grandmother, mother, a nanny. and from Italian friends went far beyond the mere chemistry of a recipe. Now, in turn, I am sharing these secrets with my own daughters, my students, and with this book I am able to let you in on some of these Italian secrets.

I was brought up in Milan. The last of five children I was born ten years after my older sister and was always considered the baby by my siblings. My grandmother, who brought me up while my mother was raising a family, was from a wealthy Jewish family from Cuneo a little town in Piedmont. She married a young and handsome Sicilian man and, as an adult, converted to Catholicism. Grandma's cooking was a combination of Piedmontese recipes and Sicilian ones. Piedmont is far to the north of Italy and Sicily is in the very south, so you can appreciate how varied her cooking was, and the breadth of experience she was able to pass on to me.

On the other side of the family, my father was a true Bolognese. Bologna is the cradle of egg pasta, of Bolognese sauce, and many other well-known Italian dishes. The summers we spent in Riccione. on the Adriatic coast of Italy, where we still have a villa, and so I saw a lot of competition in the kitchen: on one side, my mother and grandmother with their north-south traditions, and on the other side, my father's sister, with her classic Bolognese cooking. I was right in the middle of it and learned a lot from everybody!

When I married my first husband, I had the great fortune to spend a lot of time in the kitchen with his nanny, Giuditta, who was the most extraordinary cook I ever met. Her recipes seemed to be surrounded by a magical aura, and fortunately, before she passed away, I managed to jot them down. I use them even today.

I still go to Bologna, to Sicily, to Piedmont, and each time I come back with a new recipe. Each hides a secret and that is what makes cooking so much fun. The success of a recipe does not depend on a religious devotion to the instructions; it springs from the heart and requires enthusiasm and a genuine love of food. Hundreds of people have visited my kitchen to cook and share a meal with me. They left with smiles on their faces and took with them much more than the recipes. They experienced the pleasure of creating something special and of sharing a love of cooking with me and. then at home with their families and friends. They learned that good cooking goes beyond the mere chemistry of a recipe, that it is about creating a unique set of flavours, textures and a presentation that is pleasant to the palate and makes one feel good. And they took the secrets which are behind each success in the kitchen, those little tips that come from experience and love, the hints I learned from my grandmother and mother and which are part of my heritage.

Recipes are available in hundreds of cookery books. My aim is to give you more than a list of fine ingredients and a thorough description of how to put them together. I want to impart the experience that will make you a successful cook and give you pleasure in the kitchen and at the table. Here you will find the well-guarded secrets of the cooks from whom I learned the dishes, and discover which recipes I have successfully used for special family occasions, and which ones bring back happy memories for me and those I love.

In Italian cooking, the ingredients may change, but the method is always the same. For example, minestrone, Tuscan bean soup and asparagus soup all start the same way. If you can prepare one, you can prepare the others, and perhaps will go on to create your own recipe for a soup. However, please be careful with your choice of ingredients. Italian cooking is in many ways straightforward and appears simple, but this seems to invite people to take liberties with the traditional flavours that have been established over hundreds of years. I have seen top chefs demonstrating 'potato gnocchi with coconut milk sauce' and Italian meatballs with ginger'. Interesting? Possibly, but certainly not Italian.

Meanwhile, another important factor in creating the best recipes is to use the best ingredients. In The Italian Larder, I explain what are some of the key foods that are used in the Italian kitchen, why they are vital to create the most authentic dish or what they can be substituted for, if not. Use this as a guide to your cooking.

The recipes I have collected and developed are faithful to the true Italian tradition and expression of taste. My ambition is that, through this book, you will have made a new friend in me, Anna Venturi, and that together we can make your life easier and your cooking more joyful. At the end of a long day, in half an hour, we can put together a lovely meal and you will gather around the dinner table with your delighted family. You can make this happen with my Italian Secrets!

The Italian Larder

Balsamic vinegar

You might be surprised to hear that balsamic vinegar is classified by Italian law as a condiment, not a vinegar. There is a lot of misinformation about it, and on most supermarket shelves nowadays you can find bottles of mass-produced 'balsamic vinegar' that are not the real thing. True 'aceto balsamico tradizionale' is made from Trebbiano grape must (the residue of the grapes after pressing). It is simmered down until concentrated, then aged in open casks for at least twelve years. This is why it is so dear! The result of this ageing process is a thick, dark, sticky syrup to be used sparingly on salads or meat.

Mass-produced balsamic is made from a blend of cooked must, wine vinegar and, sometimes, caramel, then aged for an unspecified length of time. The difference between the two is enormous, however, for everyday use, a good mass-produced balsamic performs well without costing a fortune.

One secret to remember: never cook balsamic vinegar; just add it to your dish before going to the table.

Eggs and nuts

Several Italian dishes use raw eggs. There have been a number of food scares about eggs over the last ten years. Salmonella is a worry: the last piece of information we have is that one egg in every 700 might contain the salmonella bacteria. Each of us must make our own decision about whether or not we want to consume raw eggs. The elderly, pregnant and convalescent people should be extra careful and avoid these recipes.

The same applies to nuts, as so many 'new' nut allergies have been identified in the last few years. If you have concerns about raw eggs or nuts, watch out for recipes which include them!

Herbs

Herbs are of paramount importance In Italian cookery. If you are having trouble finding fresh herbs, do not despair. Basil, sage, and parsley all freeze very well and do not lose any of their fragrance. In summertime, at the peak of the season, I freeze a very large bag of basil so that I can use it all through the winter. Wipe the leaves with a cloth and pop them in a clear plastic bag in the deep freezer. Once frozen, quickly press down on them while they are still inside the bag. They turn almost to dust and take up a lot less room in the freezer.

There is an Italian saying to describe a person who sticks her nose in every corner: 'lei e' come il prezzemolo' (she is like parsley). This tells you that parsley is a herb that goes almost everywhere. Always keep some in your freezer and treat it like basil. The same applies to fresh sage, only there is no need to break the leaves in the bag. As you need some, take them out and in a few minutes they will come back to life, as if they were still fresh.

Rosemary, unfortunately, does not freeze well. Dried rosemary is quite acceptable, however, as the plant grows throughout the year, even during frosts, it is a good idea to keep a pot of fresh rosemary in the garden.

Mortadella

A cooked pork product with pieces of lard, nutmeg and other spices mixed into it, mortadella has a very distinctive, but not strong flavour. It can be sliced and served like other delicatessen meats or used in cooking, for example in stuffings and meatballs. If you cannot find mortadella, any good cooked ham, possibly one that is a bit fatty, makes a good substitute, especially if you add a pinch of nutmeg to the recipe.

Pancetta

'Pancia' means 'belly' and pancetta is the belly of pork, cured and sometimes smoked. It is preferable to buy pancetta in a piece, rather than thinly sliced as some supermarkets sell it, because in cooking it is generally used diced. Thin slices just do not give the same result. If you cannot find the real thing, streaky bacon is an acceptable substitute but ask your butcher to cut it in a whole piece.

Parmesan cheese

This is the king of Italian cheeses. It is used in almost every pasta dish, except those based on fish. There are two kinds of Parmesan: Parmigiano Reggiano and Grana Padano. The first is matured for at least 24 months and is produced in the area between Parma and Reggio Emilia. It is a superb cheese and a pillar of Italian cookery, perfect for grating and cooking or eating raw.

Grana Padano is very similar to the Reggiano and used in the same way. It is matured for only 18 months and is subsequently less expensive. Perhaps Padano is easier to slice into flakes and does not crumble as much as its older brother.

When buying Parmesan, only buy a wedge and grate it yourself. Ask for the authentic cheese. By Italian law, both Reggiano and Padano bear a trade mark on the rind which are your guarantee of quality. In buying a piece of 'Parmesan' with no mark of origin, you are bound to get a disappointing imitation of the real thing

One absolute no-no if you want to cook good Italian food is the ready-grated, so-called 'parmesan' sold at ambient temperature on supermarket shelves. It is a monstrosity that smells rancid and sour. If you cannot find the authentic fresh cheese, just leave it out, but please, do not put smelly sawdust on your lovely pasta!

Pasta

Pasta can be sold dried or fresh. I strongly believe that good quality fresh pasta is almost impossible to buy outside of Italy. Therefore, I would encourage people who do not live in Italy to buy a good quality dried egg pasta or to make their own.

Good dried pastas are made from durum wheat flour, kneaded with water or with whole eggs. The best are made by small, usually family-owned producers. Generally, the extruders used by these small companies are made of bronze, which gives the pasta a slightly coarse texture. This helps the sauce cling to the pasta and gives a better taste.

Always buy dried pasta marked 'made in Italy'. By Italian law, pasta must be manufactured using durum wheat flour; no other kind of flour is permitted. Durum wheat flour – also called semolina – has a very high gluten content, which makes the pasta elastic and firm to the bite and guarantees good quality.

Pasta made with egg and flour is generally thinner and more delicate in taste and texture than that made with flour and water. Egg pasta can be of different colours – green, red, black, and so on – depending on which extra ingredient is added to the eggs, for example spinach, tomato puree (paste) or squid ink. While these alternatives may be pleasant to the eye, they do not add any extra goodness to the dish. There are many types of pasta. Some sauces are matched perfectly to one in particular but you can experiment and use what is available to create your own dishes. Names and shapes change from region to region.

If you want to make your own pasta, look for an Italian flour called '00' (double zero). It is a very refined flour with a high gluten content. The resulting dough is easy to knead and will produce a springy, elastic pasta. Pasta machines are widely available nowadays and include clear instructions on how to make pasta. They are rather like a mini-mangle, as the dough is passed between two stainless steel cylinders. By gradually reducing the gap between the cylinders, you can flatten the pasta sheet until it is very thin. When the sheet of pasta is ready, it is cut into shapes, but only flat ones: tubular pasta cannot be made at home.

Prosciutto

In Italian the word prosciutto means 'ham' and does not refer to a particular variety, so products sold as prosciutto may be raw, cured or cooked. Air-cured ham is made throughout Italy but the best-known production area is Parma (in the UK Parma ham is often called 'prosciutto', using the Italian generic name). If you are looking for an air-cured ham, there is no need to go out of your way to find prosciutto di Parma. A San Daniele (from the north), or Carpegna (from the Apennines) will also be good. Cooked Italian ham is very similar to the cooked ham found in the UK and US, Some Italian food stores sell it, but it is not as popular in Italy as the air-cured variety.

Rice

Italian rice is starchy: its grain has a cloudy look, in contrast with the translucent grains, with a lower starch content, typical of Asia. Amongst Italian rices, there are several varieties that are more suitable for some recipes than others. The most common varieties are arborio, vialone nano, and carnaroli. These are available in most Italian food shops and some supermarkets.

Beware of rice that is labelled 'risotto rice'. This specification is meaningless. Risotto is a way of cooking Italian rice, it is not a variety! In a box of 'risotto rice', you are likely to find a mix of second quality rices that will not give good results when cooked.

Vialone nano, with its plump, short grains, is excellent at absorbing flavours. It has a good yield in cooking. Carnaroli is also considered a fine rice with good cooking qualities, and is ideal for risottos, timbales and salads. Personally, I like arborio and have recommended this in most recipes because it behaves well, but you can use other types if available. Arborio, the variety most loved by Italians, is a very small grain. It is ideal for risottos, where the heat penetrates the exterior of the grain, while the nucleus, which is rich in starch, remains 'al dente'.

Tomato sauce

There are so many things to know about tomato sauce one could write a book solely on it. It is important to know how the flavours work for a good tomato sauce If made with fresh tomatoes they must be very ripe, very red, and not from a greenhouse. If tomatoes of this quality are not available, please use the tinned ones instead as they probably have been harvested and preserved at their best.

Amongst tinned tomatoes, the choice is very wide: peeled whole plum tomatoes, chopped, sieved. . . they are the same, only the texture changes. Sieved tomatoes, from which the seeds have been discarded, are also called passata, which in Italian means 'sieved' Choose according to your taste, bearing in mind that the cheaper the brand, the poorer the quality is likely to be.

Stay away from tinned tomatoes with added herbs, as their flavours can be confused and not 'clean'. Sun-dried tomatoes and concentrated tomato puree (paste) should also not be used in a classic Italian tomato sauce, although they can be useful in certain recipes, as you will see.

Always bear in mind that tomatoes should not be cooked too long as they will lose their fresh, fragrant flavour. Some tomatoes whether fresh or tinned, release a lot of water while cooking. In this case you can simmer them gently with no lid on the pan. If you are using canned plum tomatoes, remember to just use the tomatoes and discard the juices that you find in the tin. If you are using fresh tomatoes and they become very watery as they start cooking simply dram and discard most of the watery juices.

Some chopped onion and/or finely chopped garlic gently fried in the oil is enough to give a good base to the sauce, providing that the tomatoes used are of very good quality. When the tomatoes are lacking in flavour, a small amount of celery and carrots, fried with the onions, will improve the flavour. Carrots, being sweet, can balance the acidity of some tinned tomatoes. Alternatively add a pinch of sugar while the sauce is cooking.

Basil is always added to the sauce, both during the cooking and at the end. It is the perfect herb to marry with tomatoes and should never be left out. It provides the essential last flavour for creating the most delicious and authentic flavour, but it must be fresh.

Vegetables

I remember my grandmother shelling peas. She would sit in her director's chair in the garden in Riccione. On her lap, in her apron, was a mountain of pea pods. There was a large bowl to one side, and, as she was telling me stories, the small tender peas were falling in the bowl. We would have the first fresh peas on Easter day, with milk-fed lamb and roast potatoes, a recipe that you can recreate here in this book.

Nowadays, frozen peas are the answer. Perhaps not as romantic, but so much easier, and still delicious. I feel comfortable buying frozen peas as long as I choose the smallest.

Spinach is another vegetable that is excellent when frozen and makes a terrific stand-by. Unless you are going to serve spinach as a side vegetable, you can use frozen spinach with confidence, blanched and squeezed to get rid of the excess water. To my mind, unlike peas and spinach, other vegetables tend to become soggy as they thaw.

You will find dishes flavoured with a host of delicious vegetables within this book, including mushrooms, courgettes, peppers and potatoes. Some are used to provide flavour and texture to a pasta sauce while others make up a classic Italian side dish.

A note about equipment

While I do not encourage people to spend extra money on kitchen tools, the correct equipment does make life easier and more enjoyable in the kitchen. After all, kitchen tools are toys for grown ups and we should enjoy them! I think a food processor and an electric whisk are indispensible and I always say that I would never have started teaching cookery without these essential tools. Remember too that a blunt knife is more dangerous than a sharp one.

Unless you are baking a cake, or you are preparing a soufflé, a religious following of quantities is unnecessary to good cooking.

Soups

Preparing soups

In Italy, we tend to serve soup for supper, to prepare the stomach for the rest of the meal. On a cold winter evening, a warm soup is particularly welcome.

The method of preparing Italian soups is always the same and there are three stages to be followed. Start the soup with a few vegetables gently sautéed in oil or butter until golden. They will produce a lovely deep taste that is the backdrop of the soup.

The second stage is to add the other ingredients to the pan and allow them to release their flavours and moisture while cooking, until they have become golden. This results in all the flavours blending together nicely.

Then it is time to add water or stock and cook the soup further. The thickened base from stage two will be diluted with the stock, and you can control how liquid you want your soup to be.

Soup can rest in the fridge for up to four days. When reheated, the taste improves.

Pasta e Fagioli

Italian bean soup

The beans I use for this soup are far superior to the canned beans in your local supermarket, so you will get fantastic results. The ideal variety is dried borlotti, which are also known as cranberry beans, although they have nothing to do with cranberries.

Place the dried beans in a bowl, cover with plenty of cold water and leave to soak overnight; they will double in volume.

In a soup pot or deep saucepan, heat the olive oil and sauté the vegetables and garlic until they start to brown.

Drain and rinse the beans and add them to the vegetables. Cover immediately with cold water. Add the rosemary, tomato purée (paste), and simmer gently for about 2 hours until the beans are tender.

Drain half the bean-vegetable mixture and pass it through a mouli-légumes to remove the skin of the beans. Leave the remaining beans whole to give texture to the soup.

Return the puréed and whole beans to the pot. Add water to thin the soup to the desired consistency.

In a separate saucepan, cook the pasta according to the packet instructions, then drain and stir it into the soup. Season to taste.

Serve with Parmesan cheese, freshly ground pepper and a drizzle of extra virgin olive oil.

Serves 6–8

500 g/1 lb/2½ cups dried borlotti (cranberry) beans

5 tbsp extra virgin olive oil, plus extra to serve

1 small onion, chopped

1 small carrot, chopped

2 sticks celery, chopped

2 cloves garlic, chopped

2 sprigs rosemary

2 tbsp concentrated tomato purée (paste)

100 g/3½ oz/1 cup small pasta, such as ditalini

3 tbsp Parmesan cheese, grated

My Secrets

When cooking dried beans, remember that salt should never be added while cooking, only at the end, and beans should always start cooking in cold water. This will prevent the skin from getting tough and peeling off.

It is best to use a mouli-légumes to purée the beans and remove the skins – a blender won't do the job properly.

The soup (without the pasta) can be prepared in advance, but the pasta must be added just before serving. The perfect pasta shape for this soup is called ditalini. It looks like a small maccheroni but is only 1 cm/½ in long.

Minestrone alla Milanese

Mixed vegetable soup

Serves 8–10

5 tbsp extra virgin olive oil, plus extra to serve

1 medium onion, diced

2 cloves garlic, chopped

3 sticks celery, diced

2 carrots, diced

2 courgettes (zucchini)

120 g/4 oz/1½ cups french beans (haricots verts)

120 g/4 oz/1½ cups peas

3–4 leaves savoy cabbage

1 x 240 g/8 oz can plum tomatoes

1 large potato, diced

150 g/5 oz/¾ cup tinned borlotti (cranberry) beans

2 tbsp arborio rice per person

3 tbsp basil, chopped

3 tbsp parsley, chopped

salt and pepper

Parmesan cheese, grated, to serve

Minestrone is particularly good in summer when fresh, fragrant vegetables are available in the market. Made without the rice, it can also be blended to a lovely cream of vegetable soup.

In a soup pot or deep saucepan, heat the olive oil and sauté the onion, garlic, celery and carrots for a few minutes.

Meanwhile, dice the courgettes (zucchini) and french beans (haricots verts), shell the peas and cut the cabbage leaves into strips, gradually adding them to the pot as you prepare them. Add the plum tomatoes, but not the potato. Continue sautéing the vegetables for 15 minutes.

Add enough water to just cover the vegetables. Lower the heat and simmer the soup for 1 hour.

Add more water to thin the soup to the desired consistency. Add the potato and the drained borlotti (cranberry) beans and cook for 10 minutes, or until the potato is tender but not mushy.

Meanwhile, in a separate saucepan, boil just enough rice for the number of people you are serving.

When the potato is tender, turn off the heat under the soup. Add the chopped basil and parsley to the soup and stir thoroughly.

When the rice is al dente, drain and divide it amongst the serving bowls. Add the soup and stir well.

Serve each bowl with a sprinkling of extra virgin olive oil, salt and ground pepper and grated Parmesan cheese.

My Secrets

This soup is very tasty when prepared one day in advance, stored in the fridge and then reheated.

For the best flavour, it is important that the vegetables should be thoroughly sautéed in the oil before you add any water.

Cooking only the necessary amount of rice for each person and reserving the leftover soup is a good way to ensure that the rice is always al dente. When rice is reheated it overcooks. Left over Parmesan rind, scraped with a knife to remove the outer wax, is delicious cooked in the soup.

Zuppa di Funghi, Rustica

Rustic soup with mushrooms

An unusual soup but delicious and quite easy to prepare, this is perfect as a starter on a cold autumn evening. The recipe comes from my friend Elena, a 'miracle cook', who can put together a delicious meal for 12 or more in just an hour. It is important to use a crusty bread and very fresh, fragrant parsley.

Prepare the mushrooms as in the recipe for Funghi Trifolati (Sautéed mushrooms) on page 99, and reserve.

Bring the stock to a boil, add the wine and simmer for 15 minutes.

In the meantime, break the eggs into a bowl and beat them with a fork. Mix in the Parmesan cheese and parsley and set aside.

Stir the sautéed mushrooms into the boiling stock. Add the egg mixture, stirring quickly with a fork to prevent lumps.

Place a piece of toasted crusty bread in each serving bowl and ladle over the boiling hot soup.

Serves 6–8

1 kg/2¼ lb/5 cups chestnut mushrooms, sliced

30 g/1 oz/2 level tbsp dried wild mushrooms

3 vegetable stock cubes, to make 1.5 litres/2½ pints/ 2 quarts stock

600 ml/1 pint/2½ cups dry white wine

6 large eggs

150 g/5 oz/¾ cup Parmesan cheese, grated

2 tbsp parsley, chopped

6–8 large slices crusty bread, about 1 cm/½ in thick, toasted

My Secrets

This soup is even better when the mushrooms have been prepared in advance, as the flavour of the dried mushrooms permeates the fresh ones. Also Italian stock cubes will further enhance the taste.

If you want to give the soup an even more rustic flavour, rub a peeled garlic clove on the toasted bread as soon as it comes out of the toaster. The hot bread will 'melt' the garlic and lend a distinctive garlic flavour to the soup.

Vellutata di Asparagi coi Crostini

Smooth asparagus soup with croûtons

Serves 6

1 kg/2 lb/5 cups
asparagus, fresh or frozen

90 g/3 oz/⅓ cup butter

1 medium onion, chopped

2 leeks, chopped

1 stick celery, chopped

2 cloves garlic

1 large potato, peeled and
chopped

salt and pepper

2 vegetable or chicken
stock cubes, to make 1
litre/2 pints/5 cups stock

4 tbsp single (light) cream

3 tbsp Parmesan cheese,
freshly grated

1 baguette, stale

extra virgin olive oil, to
drizzle

salt and pepper

*'Vellutata' in Italian means velvety, so the texture of this, or any other
soup made with vegetables and blended, should be velvety and
smooth. This soup is delicious made with fresh asparagus in season,
but frozen spears are a good alternative.*

Wash the asparagus and discard the tough ends. Cut off the fresh
tips and reserve. Chop the rest of the asparagus roughly.

Melt most of the butter in a soup pot or large saucepan. Add
the onion, leeks, celery and garlic and cook over medium heat for
about 10 minutes or until they are softened.

Add the chopped asparagus spears and the potato, season
with salt and pepper and cook for another 10 minutes, stirring from
time to time.

When all the vegetables are well coated with butter and have
released some moisture, add just enough of the stock to cover them.
Cook for 30 minutes or until all the vegetables are tender.

In the meantime, sauté the reserved asparagus tips in a small frying
pan with the remaining butter. When the tips are cooked but still
crunchy, remove from the heat and set aside.

In a food processor, blend the soup until smooth. Add more stock
to thin the soup to the consistency of single cream. Add the fried
asparagus tips and the cream, then the freshly grated Parmesan
cheese and stir over a medium heat until hot.

To make the croûtons, heat the oven to 180°C/350°F/Gas 4 and slice
the bread wafer thin. Working in batches, scatter the slices of bread
on a baking tray and drizzle some olive oil on top. Dry the slices in
the oven until they are golden and crunchy. Serve with the soup.

My Secrets

The secret of a good tasty soup is to allow all the ingredients to cook
well with the oil or butter until almost done, before adding any stock.
If the stock is added too soon, the vegetables end up being boiled,
which results in a very 'washed out' taste.

This is even better when made a day in advance and reheated.

If using frozen asparagus for the soup, buy just a few fresh spears
and use their tips for the garnish.

Vellutata di Cavolfiore

Creamy cauliflower soup

My grandmother used to start cooking this soup in the morning, and I would get up to the smell of cauliflower, instead of freshly made coffee and brioche. That is why, at the time, I wasn't very fond of cauliflower soup! Now, however, I must admit that it is quite delicious and delicate in taste.

Melt half the butter in a deep pan over a medium heat. Add the onion, leek and potato and cook for 10 minutes until the onion is translucent.

Add the cauliflower and cook for a further 5 minutes, tossing from time to time. Add the stock.

Simmer for 30 minutes, or until all the vegetables are soft. Leave to cool a little and transfer to a blender and purèe until smooth.

Return to the pan and bring to the boil. Adjust the seasoning to taste, add the remaining butter and serve with chopped parsley and plenty of Parmesan cheese.

Serves 6

120 g/4 oz/½ cup butter

1 small onion, chopped

1 small leek, chopped

1 large potato, peeled and cut into chunks

1 medium cauliflower, trimmed and cut into small pieces

1 litre/2 pints stock

salt and pepper

small bunch parsley, chopped, to serve

6 tbsp Parmesan cheese, grated, to serve

My Secret
Make sure that the butter does not burn and that it stays clear by keeping the heat low. This will give your soup a very delicate flavour.

Minestre di Erbe Passate

Mixed greens soup

Serves 6–8

1 bunch Swiss chard, about 5–6 leaves

1 bunch fresh spinach leaves

1 round lettuce

¼ Savoy cabbage

1 small onion, chopped

1 celery stalk, chopped

1 small bunch each parsley, basil and dill

150 g/5 oz/¾ cup butter

1 large potato, peeled and sliced

salt and pepper

800 ml–1 litre/27 fl oz–2 pints/4–5 cups stock

8–10 tbsp Parmesan cheese, grated, to serve

My grandmother was an expert soup maker. This is one of her favourites, which she liked to cook for us on a cold winter evening, served with crusty bread and lots of Parmesan cheese.

Thoroughly wash the chard, spinach, lettuce and cabbage. Chop roughly and leave to soak in clean water while you start the soup.

Chop the onion, celery, parsley, basil and dill very finely, then sauté gently with half the butter in a deep pan, until the onion is translucent.

Add the greens, still with water clinging to their leaves, and the potato. Season with salt, toss and cover with a lid. At this point, the greens will begin to wilt and release more water. Let them stew, covered, for at least 20 minutes over a low to medium heat.

Turn the heat off and transfer the greens to a blender. Purée until very smooth, then return to the pan. Add enough stock to dilute the greens into a soup consistency. Adjust the seasoning, then simmer for a further 15 minutes.

Just before serving, add the remaining butter, then serve piping hot, with plenty of crusty bread and Parmesan cheese.

My Secret
Remember to season the greens with salt as they go into the pan; this will fix the chlorophyll and keep the soup bright green.

Vellutata al Cerfoglio

Cream of watercress soup

In Italy, watercress is considered a delicacy and it is not as well-known as in Britain. This recipe is from my mother's collection and was served whenever she wanted to impress a sophisticated guest.

Wash the watercress thoroughly, discarding the thick stems.

Bring a large pan of salted water to the boil and cook the watercress for 2–3 minutes. Drain, then transfer to a bowl of cold water to retain its green colour. Drain again, squeeze well with your hands and dry with a towel to remove all the water.

Chop the watercress, then transfer it to a blender, adding the butter. Process until the mixture is very finely chopped to almost a paste.

Prepare a small quantity of Besciamella. Melt the butter, stir in the flour and cook for 1 minute. Slowly add the hot milk, then cook for at least 10 minutes over a very low heat. Allow the sauce to cool.

Mix the watercress with the cooled Besciamella, tossing well with a spoon or a whisk. Add the piping hot stock and serve warm with some crostini.

Serves 6

For the soup:

4 bunches watercress

salt and pepper

60 g/2 oz/¼ cup butter

1 litre/2 pints/5 cups meat stock (see recipe on page 25)

For the Besciamella (béchamel) sauce:

2–3 tbsp butter

2–3 tbsp plain (all-purpose) flour

200 ml/7 fl oz/1 cup whole milk, heated

My Secret

The watercress must be squeezed very well, then puréed to a very, very fine texture in order to achieve a velvety smooth consistency. This soup is perfect if you can't see any bits of cress! If you don't have a blender, pass the soup through a very fine sieve.

Zuppa di Cozze
Mussel soup

Serves 6

1.5 kg/3 lb live mussels

3 anchovies

1 bunch parsley

3 cloves garlic

180 ml/6 fl oz/2½ cups dry white wine

5 tbsp extra virgin olive oil

5 tbsp canned sieved or plum tomatoes

salt and pepper

parsley, chopped, to garnish

This soup is simplicity itself! The same method can be used for clam soup, though I personally find that mussels are better because clams can release sand during cooking, ruining the final result. Mussels are excellent and, because they are farmed, they are easily available.

Wash the mussels individually under running tap water, removing all the beards from the shells.

Put the anchovies, parsley and 1 clove garlic in a food processor and chop until very fine. With the machine still running, slowly add the wine.

Place the oil and remaining whole garlic in a deep pan, then heat slowly until the garlic starts to colour. Remove the garlic and discard.

Add the anchovy sauce to the oil. Stir well, then simmer in a saucepan for a few minutes until the wine has evaporated. Add the tomatoes and 2 tbsp water. Season with salt and pepper, then cook over a medium heat for a further 5–10 minutes.

Add the mussels, cover the pan tightly with a lid, and continue to cook over a medium heat. (From time to time, holding the lid on, shake the pan up and down to move the mussels around.) Around 7–10 minutes, check that all the mussels are open, discarding any that remain closed.

Prepare individual soup bowls with crusty toasted bread, then ladle in the mussels with their sauce. Garnish with parsley to serve.

My Secret
All shellfish becomes tough and rubbery if overcoooked, so turn the heat off as soon as the shells begin to open. They are then ready to eat.

Brodo di Carne

Classic meat stock

A good meat stock will make all the difference to the outcome of your recipes. It is easy to prepare, can be frozen for any occasion and is indispensable for making good soup. To make a good meat stock, you need a selection of raw meats, though not necessarily expensive cuts, preferably beef, chicken or turkey, veal and pork – the carcass of the Christmas turkey is not suitable! There is no need to add any bones unless you have some with marrow, as this will add extra flavour to the stock. The correct proportion of meat to water is 100 g/ 4 oz meat to 1 litre/2 pints water.

Place all the meat in a large stock pot and cover with 6 litres/12 pints cold water. Add 2 tsp salt.

Start the heat as low as possible then, when the water comes to the boil, add all the remaining ingredients.

Simmer very gently for at least 2 hours, then discard all the meat and vegetables as all their goodness will now be in the stock. Adjust seasoning to taste.

If you want your stock very lean, refrigerate it. When cold, the fat on the surface will be easy to skim off with a spoon.

Makes 6 litres/10 pints stock

600 g/1¼ lb mixed meat

salt and pepper

2 cloves

1 large onion, roughly chopped

1 large carrot, roughly chopped

2 celery stalks, roughly chopped

1 small bunch parsley

My Secrets

It is essential to start the meat in cold, salted water, on an extremely low heat. This will allow the meat to release its juices into the stock, giving a better result. (If you want meat to be juicy and don't care about the stock, boil the water to seal the meat and retain its flavour.) Throw a clove or two into the stock to give extra flavour, if you like.

Do not peel the onion; its skin will give the stock an appetising golden shade.

Pasta

Cooking perfect pasta

The cooking method is an important issue when preparing pasta. You will need plenty of boiling water. As soon as the water is boiling, it needs to be salted generously; for each litre of water (about 2 pints/ 1 quart) you will need 1 teaspoon of salt. The amount of time needed to cook the pasta will depend on the shape and whether it is dried or fresh – fresh pasta cooks very quickly and only needs a few minutes in boiling water.

When the pasta is cooked, it should be drained immediately and dressed right away. Never leave your pasta 'naked' after draining. In a few minutes it will be stuck together in an awful blob! Always keep some of the cooking water and add 1 or 2 tablespoons of it to the pasta when dressing it, regardless of which sauce you use.

When cooking pasta for baked dishes (lasagne or timbales, for example), drain it a few minutes before it is completely done because the pasta will be cooked further in the oven. Remember pasta for baking should always be covered with a 'blanket' of sauce or vegetables. This will prevent the top layer from drying out in the oven.

In pasta salads, the secret of success is to rinse the cooked pasta under cold water before adding the other ingredients. This will cool the pasta and stop the cooking process. A little oil can then be used to prevent the pasta sticking together. Do not use butter as it will solidify when cool and the result will be unappetising. Also, remember that pasta salads do not keep fresh and fragrant for more than a few hours.

Orecchiette coi Broccoli
Orecchiette with broccoli

Orecchiette means 'little ears'. This pasta is typical of Apulia in the south-east of Italy. I love this recipe because it is fast, healthy, easy and inexpensive. When my girls were 4 and 5 years old, I had a nanny, Assunta, from Lecce, and she taught me how to make this delicious dish. The girls still like it so much that it is very often part of our Sunday lunch. The original recipe is made with calabrese, which in Italian is called cime di rapa. *Broccoli is a perfect alternative, not a compromise. Orecchiette also goes very well with Amatriciana (Chilli and bacon) sauce (see page 54).*

Put a large pot of water on to boil. In the meantime, in a small saucepan, heat the olive oil and gently fry the garlic and anchovies until the garlic is brown and the anchovies dissolve.

When the pot of water comes to the boil, salt it and add the broccoli. Bring back to the boil and add the orecchiette. Cook for 15–20 minutes, or until the pasta is al dente.

Drain the broccoli and pasta together and dress with the sizzling garlic-anchovy mixture, tossing gently so that everything is coated with the oil. Add the Parmesan cheese, toss again, and add the chilli.

Serves 6

5 tbsp extra virgin olive oil

2 cloves garlic, sliced

3 anchovies, packed in oil

florets from 2 large heads of broccoli

500 g/1 lb/2½ cups orecchiette

6 tbsp Parmesan cheese, grated

1 tsp crushed dried chilli

My Secrets
Use a spoon to stir the anchovies until they completely dissolve in the oil but be careful not to burn the garlic as it will lend an awful bitter taste to the oil!

Always cook broccoli in salted water to help it retain its colour.

Penne al Pomodoro e Vodka

Short pasta with tomato and vodka sauce

Serves 4–6

3 tbsp extra virgin olive oil

2 cloves garlic, chopped

1 x 250 g/9 oz can plum or chopped tomatoes

salt and pepper

6–8 basil leaves

500 g/1 lb/2½ cups dried penne

4 tbsp butter

1 tbsp crushed black pepper

150 ml/5 fl oz/⅔ cup single (light) cream

120 ml/4 fl oz/½ cup vodka

Parmesan cheese, grated, to serve

Here is a really effortless recipe, although the result is superb. Always choose a short pasta like smooth penne as it goes very well with a creamy sauce. It also makes a good starter, in which case this amount of pasta will serve six people.

To make the sauce, heat the olive oil in a small saucepan. Add the chopped garlic and fry gently until golden. Add the tomatoes and season with salt and pepper. Add the fresh basil and cook gently for about 10 minutes.

While the sauce is simmering, cook the pasta in a large pan of boiling salted water until al dente. Drain.

In a large frying pan, melt the butter, add the crushed pepper and the drained pasta. Toss well over a medium heat, making sure that all the pasta is well coated with butter.

Add the tomato sauce and cream and mix well over a high heat. Remove from the heat, sprinkle with the vodka, and toss again. Serve immediately, with Parmesan cheese handed separately.

My Secrets

The vodka in this recipe creates a flavour that is a little modern, adding some variety to the collection of recipes.

To keep that special taste that comes from the vodka, do not cook it, but add it only at the end. If you allow it to evaporate, its flavour will be lost.

Spaghetti alla Carbonara

Spaghetti with carbonara sauce

Carbonara is a very well known sauce, perhaps because it is very rich and creamy. Most supermarkets sell their own brand of carbonara, but it is not for the real Italian gourmet. Moreover, this sauce is so quick to prepare that it makes no sense to spend extra money to buy a ready-made one. I remember cooking Spaghetti alla Carbonara for my friends when I was a teenager, when my parents had gone out and left the house at our mercy. The first attempts were quite unsuccessful and the eggs scrambled, but with my secrets this will not be a problem for you.

Bring a large pot of water to the boil.

Meanwhile, break the eggs in a bowl, add the cream and the Parmesan cheese and beat together with a fork to give a rather thick sauce. Set aside.

Cut the pancetta into small cubes and fry it with the butter until crispy but not too dry. Set aside.

When the water is boiling, salt it generously and add the pasta. Stir immediately and cook until al dente.

Drain the pasta in a colander then return it to the empty pot. Pour the egg mixture on top and toss very quickly. Add the pancetta.

Decorate with parsley and freshly ground pepper (no salt is necessary as the pancetta is salty enough). Serve immediately on warm plates.

Serves 4

2 large eggs

1 tbsp single (light) cream

4 tbsp Parmesan cheese, grated

90 g/3 oz/½ cup pancetta

2 tbsp butter

500 g/1 lb/2½ cups spaghetti or spaghettini

1 tbsp parsley, finely chopped (optional)

pepper

My Secrets
The heat of the drained pasta alone is not enough to cook the raw eggs. Some people sauté the dressed spaghetti in a frying pan to make sure that the eggs cook: the result is not Carbonara but spaghetti with scrambled eggs! Others dress the spaghetti directly in the serving dish, giving a very wet carbonara. The solution is dressing the pasta in the same pot in which the spaghetti has been cooking. This gives just enough heat to cook the eggs without any risk of ruining the final result.

In case you find that the pasta is still too wet, sprinkle it with some more Parmesan cheese to absorb extra moisture.

Linguine al Pesto

Linguine with pesto

Serves 4–6

For the sauce:

2 large handfuls basil leaves, about 40 leaves

4–6 cloves garlic

5 tbsp Parmesan cheese, grated, plus extra to garnish

3 tbsp pine kernels, toasted

salt, to taste

5 tbsp Ligurian extra virgin olive oil

1 tbsp salt

500 g/1 lb/2½ cups linguine

100 g/3½ oz/½ cup fine French beans (haricots verts), trimmed

1 small potato, peeled and sliced

Pesto is typical of Liguria in the northwest of Italy. The best basil for this recipe is the Ligurian basil, which has a small leaf, very strong flavour and no minty taste. The best season for it is summer – that anaemic basil you grow with so much love on your window sill in winter will not do the job. The quality of the oil used to blend the ingredients together is also important as it must have a gentle and mild taste. Try to use a Ligurian oil which will not overpower the basil. The moral of the story is that the pesto you make at home is never as good as the one you find in Liguria. However, if you follow this recipe, you will make a pesto at least a hundred times better than the supermarket version! The traditional method of making pesto requires a pestle and mortar (from which comes the name 'pesto'), but you can achieve good results with a food processor.

To make the sauce, place the basil, garlic, Parmesan cheese, toasted pine kernels and 1 teaspoon of salt in a food processor. Switch it on and gradually pour in the oil in a very thin stream. Stop pouring when the sauce becomes a thick paste.

Bring a pot with 5 litres/10 pints/5 quarts of water to a boil. When boiling, add 1 tablespoon of salt and then add the linguine, beans and sliced potato all together. Stir with a fork and cook in fiercely boiling water for 7–10 minutes or until the pasta is al dente – taste to check that it is cooked.

Drain the pasta and vegetables and dress immediately with the pesto. Serve with extra Parmesan cheese to taste.

My Secrets

Keep a couple of tablespoons of the water in which the pasta has been cooking to thin the sauce. This will make it easier to dress the pasta, and the outcome will be more moist.

Pesto can freeze well without losing its freshness.

Don't wash the basil in water as this will spoil the taste. Instead, wipe the leaves with a cloth.

Linguine with Pesto (page 32)

Orecchiette with Broccoli (page 29) and Potato Dumplings with Butter and Fried Sage (page 38)

Chicken Stuffed with Pine Kernels and Pistachio Nuts (page 80) and Raw Artichoke Salad with Parmesan Cheese (page 114)

Saffron Pasta Salad (page 117) and Tuscan Bean Salad (page 115)

Risotto with Prawns, Cream and Brandy (page 66)

Capelli d'Angelo al Pomodoro e Scampi

Angel hair pasta with tomato, prawns and herbs

Angel hair, being a delicate, thin pasta, goes very well with the sweet flavours of prawns and tomato. In supermarkets you can find raw, shelled prawns (shrimp) which are grey, or precooked prawns which are pink. For this recipe I recommend you use the raw prawns, as you can more easily control the cooking time. Always remember that shellfish, if overdone, become rubbery.

To peel the tomatoes, bring a pot of water to a boil and immerse the tomatoes, one at a time, for a few seconds in the boiling water. Transfer the scalded tomatoes to a bowl of cold water to cool quickly. Slip off the skins and cut the flesh into 2.5 cm/1 in chunks, discarding the seeds.

Heat the oil in a large frying pan. Sauté the garlic over a medium heat until golden. Add the chopped tomatoes all in one go, raise the heat to maximum and keep tossing until they start to mush.

Add the prawns (shrimp) and chopped herbs to the sauce and cook, tossing quickly, until the prawns turn pink. Season with salt and pepper. Your sauce is now ready.

Bring some water for the pasta to the boil. Salt generously and cook the pasta until al dente. Drain, remembering to keep some of the water.

Add the pasta to the sauce in the frying pan and toss gently. If the pasta looks too wet, turn the heat on for a moment – it will dry out quickly, as the pasta keeps absorbing the water. Alternatively, you may need to add some of the water that you reserved. Pour into a serving dish and serve immediately, without Parmesan cheese!

Serves 6

10 medium tomatoes, ripe but firm

8 tbsp extra virgin olive oil

2–3 cloves garlic, sliced

500 g/1 lb/2½ cups king prawns (shrimp), shelled

1 tbsp basil, chopped

1 tbsp parsley, chopped

salt and pepper

500 g/1 lb/2½ cups angel hair pasta or tagliolini

My Secrets

When cooking angel hair, it is best to use a pasta pan. This is a pot into which a deep colander fits. When draining the pasta, you have only to lift the colander, with the pasta in it, out of the larger pot, leaving all the cooking water still in the pot.

The quality of the tomatoes makes a big difference to the outcome of this dish. Some release more water than others. To reduce the tomato juices without overcooking the tomato flesh, remove the pieces from the frying pan with a skimmer or slotted spoon and simmer the juices only. Then put the pieces back in the pan and toss with the pasta.

pasta 33

Maccheroni ai Quattro Formaggi

Four cheese macaroni

Serves 6–8

1 litre/2 pints/5 cups Besciamella sauce (see page 47)

500 g/1 lb/2½ cups tortiglioni

100 g/3½ oz/½ cup gorgonzola cheese, diced

100 g/3½ oz/½ cup mozzarella cheese, diced

100 g/3½ oz/½ cup fontina cheese, diced

4 tbsp Parmesan cheese, grated

The Italian version of macaroni cheese, this is the dish I fed my daughters when, like most children, they were making a fuss about eating. We were calling it pasta con la crostina, crostina *being the grilled, golden top. Bake the pasta in a hot oven until the top has a nice golden crust and is bubbling. This dish freezes very well and is ideal to have ready when you are having a late supper.*

Make the Besciamella sauce.

Lightly cook the pasta in plenty of salted boiling water, until very al dente, remembering it will cook in the oven as well. Drain the pasta and dress it with two-thirds of the Besciamella sauce.

Preheat the oven to 180°C/350°F/Gas 4. Spread out half your pasta in an ovenproof dish and dot half of each of the diced cheeses over it. Place the rest of the pasta on top and then sprinkle with the remaining diced cheeses.

Cover the dish completely with the rest of the Besciamella and sprinkle the Parmesan cheese on top. Bake for 25–30 minutes and serve immediately.

My Secrets

Putting small pieces of cheese here and there on the pasta is delicious, because when eating, you come across the different tastes and textures of the cheeses. Do not put all the cheeses into the Besciamella as they will melt together, making the sauce heavy.

Use a tubular pasta such as maccheroni, tortiglioni or penne: the sauce will fill the tubes, making it a very moist dish. Choose your cheeses with care too: you need to achieve balance between a strong cheese, a mild one, and one that melts well.

Timballini degli Angeli

Angel timbales

Timbales are baked moulds that can be made of pasta or rice. These mini-versions are best served with a delicious home-made tomato sauce. They make a light main course when accompanied by a salad. I call them 'angel' because they are very delicate and made with angel hair pasta.

Prepare 6 individual moulds of 150 ml/5 fl oz/⅔ cup capacity by buttering them thickly and carefully coating the insides with the breadcrumbs. This will prevent the pasta sticking to the moulds.

Make the Besciamella sauce and set aside. Bring a pot of water to a boil, salt it and cook the pasta until very al dente, remembering it will cook in the oven as well. Dress the pasta with the Besciamella, and toss well, making sure that all the Besciamella is mixed with the pasta.

Preheat the oven to 180°C/350°F/Gas 4. Half-fill the moulds with the dressed pasta, leaving a well in the centre. Fill with some of the diced cheese and ham, then fill each mould to the rim with the remaining pasta.

Bake for 15–20 minutes. To unmould the timbales, run a knife around the inside of the moulds to detach the timbales and turn out onto serving plates. Serve hot, while the cheese is still melting, on a bed of tomato sauce.

Serves 6

about 2 tbsp butter, for greasing

about 30 g/ 1 oz/2 level tbsp fine breadcrumbs, for coating

500 ml/1 pint/2½ cups Besciamella sauce (see page 47)

170 g/6 oz/¾ cup angel hair pasta or tagliolini

120 g/4 oz/½ cup fontina cheese, diced

120 g/4 oz/½ cup cooked ham, diced

My Secret
Fontina cheese is not always available, but you can replace it with a semi-mature cheese such as Raclette.

Timballo di Maccheroni ai Funghi Porcini

Wild mushrooms timbale

Serves 6–8

30 g/1 oz/2 level tbsp dried wild mushrooms

500 g/1 lb/2¾ cups chestnut mushrooms

3 cloves garlic, sliced

5 tbsp extra virgin olive oil

salt and pepper

1 tbsp parsley, chopped

1 litre/2 pints/5 cups Besciamella sauce (see page 47)

500 g/1 lb/2½ cups penne or maccheroni

4 tbsp Parmesan cheese, grated

In this recipe, the delicious strong flavour of the mushrooms blends very well with the Besciamella sauce and Parmesan cheese. The dish you use should be ovenproof and deep, like a soufflé dish.

In a small bowl, soak the dried mushrooms covered in 300 ml/10 fl oz/1¼ cups of hot water for at least 30 minutes. Meanwhile, clean and slice the fresh mushrooms. Set aside.

In a frying pan, sauté the garlic in the olive oil. Add the fresh mushrooms and sauté for a few minutes until they wilt. Lift the dried mushrooms from their soaking water and add them to the pan. Cook, stirring gently, for 3–5 minutes.

Strain the soaking water through a muslin cloth or kitchen paper and add it to the frying pan. Cover and simmer very gently until all the water evaporates. Season with salt, pepper and plenty of chopped fresh parsley.

Make the Besciamella sauce. Meanwhile, in a large pot with plenty of boiling, salted water, cook the pasta until very al dente. Drain a couple of minutes before it is fully cooked and dress with half the Besciamella sauce. Add half of the cooked mushroom mixture and toss gently.

Preheat the oven to 180°C/350°F/Gas 4. Put half the dressed pasta in the serving dish and place the remaining mushrooms in the centre of the dish. Cover with the rest of the pasta and pour the remaining Besciamella on top.

Sprinkle with the Parmesan cheese and bake for 35 minutes or until a golden crust forms on the top. Serve immediately.

My Secrets

Fresh mushrooms should not be washed, just wiped with a damp cloth, as they will turn soggy if put under water.

When pouring the Besciamella sauce over the finished dish, use a fork or a spoon to encourage it to soak into the pasta. On serving, it will be wonderfully moist, with the Besciamella filling the gaps in the pasta.

An advantage of all timbales is that they don't require any care before serving; they can be prepared in advance and baked at the last minute, making them a good choice for entertaining. This one can also be frozen before baking.

Crespelle con Ricotta e Spinaci

Pancakes with spinach and ricotta

Thin pancakes are very popular in Italy and so there are many different ways to fill a pancake. Spinach and ricotta is a classic combination with the advantage that you can use frozen chopped spinach instead of fresh. It can be prepared in two stages, first the pancakes and then the filling. The assembly takes only a few minutes and there is no risk of failing.

Put the flour in a bowl and break the eggs onto the flour. With a fork, start mixing, adding the milk little by little. Don't be tempted to use an electric whisk or the batter will be gluey. If any lumps form, pass the batter through a sieve. Just before cooking, add the oil and stir well. Thin the batter with 2 ladles of cold water.

Heat a non-stick frying pan about 18 cm/7 in in diameter. Check that it is hot enough by dropping a little batter into the pan. If it solidifies immediately, it is ready. Cook each pancake on one side well first, then turn over with a spatula and finish on the other side. Slide onto a plate and repeat with the remaining batter.

To prepare the filling, in a frying pan over a medium heat, sauté the frozen spinach and garlic in half the butter for 20 minutes or until the water has completely evaporated. Leave the lid on the pan at first, to help the spinach thaw, then cook uncovered.

With a fork, mix the ricotta cheese and the Parmesan cheese into the spinach. Season with nutmeg, salt and pepper. Fill each pancake with a tablespoon of the mixture and roll up or fold.

Preheat the oven to 180°C/350°F/Gas 4. Melt the remaining butter. Lay the crespelle in an ovenproof serving dish and brush with the melted butter. Sprinkle with the extra Parmesan cheese and the pine kernels and bake for 15 minutes until the nuts are toasted and crunchy. Serve immediately.

Serves 6

For the pancakes:

240 g/8 oz/1¼ cups plain (all-purpose) white flour

3 medium eggs

600 ml/1 pint/2½ cups milk

5 tbsp vegetable oil

For the filling:

1 kg/2 lb/5 cups frozen chopped spinach

2–3 cloves garlic

120 g/4 oz/½ cup butter

250 g/9 oz/1 heaping cup ricotta cheese

5 tbsp Parmesan cheese, grated, plus extra to garnish

a pinch of nutmeg

salt and pepper

2 tbsp pine kernels

My Secrets

Before cooking, let the batter rest for at least an hour, or even overnight. Adding a couple of ladles of cold water will make your pancakes thinner and crispier.

Adding the oil to the batter is a terrific trick to avoid greasing the pan after each pancake but it is crucial to use a non-stick pan. I like the teflon-coated ones.

The batter should make about 20 pancakes. You can freeze the leftovers easily. Just stack the pancakes on top of each other and cover with plastic wrap.

Gnocchi di Patate al Burro e Salvia

Potato dumplings with butter and fried sage

Serves 6

1 kg/2 lb/5 cups potatoes

200–300 g/7–10 oz/1–1½ cups Italian '00' or plain (all-purpose) white flour

salt

4–5 leaves fresh sage

120 g/4 oz/½ cup butter

5 tbsp Parmesan cheese, grated

Gnocchi, a speciality of northern Italy, is a nice alternative to pasta. You will have excellent results using any kind of sauce, as long as it is runny. They are very good served with a casserole or beef stew. Try them with tomato sauce and plenty of Parmesan, some pesto, ragu' or a gorgonzola sauce. Remember that gnocchi are delicate and cannot be tossed or they will break. The only disadvantage of this dish is that gnocchi must be cooked soon after they are prepared or they become gluey.

Boil the unpeeled potatoes in plenty of water until tender – for medium-sized potatoes, 40–45 minutes should be enough. Drain and peel them while still very hot.

Using a ricer, mash the potatoes immediately onto the kitchen counter and add the flour and a pinch of salt. Mix gently with your hands to a soft dough, adding more flour if necessary.

Shape the dough into long rolls as thick as a thumb and cut them into 2.5 cm/1 in segments. Place them on a tray or the kitchen table and sprinkle with plenty of flour to prevent sticking. To move them, use a spatula, so as not to mash them.

Bring a large pot of water to the boil, add salt, and cook the gnocchi in batches so you do not overcrowd the pan and make them stick together. The gnocchi are cooked when they rise to the surface: it takes less than 1 minute. Using a slotted ladle, remove them from the water and place in a warm serving dish. Proceed until all the gnocchi are cooked.

In the meantime, fry the sage in the butter until golden, then pour the sizzling, foaming butter onto the cooked gnocchi. Sprinkle with Parmesan cheese and serve immediately.

My Secrets

The kind of potatoes you use will make a difference. King Edward or Desirée potatoes give very good results.

When boiling the potatoes, make sure they do not break or overcook. They will absorb too much water and this will require extra flour to hold the dough together, making the gnocchi tough.

Mix the mashed potatoes with the flour while still hot. The steam will be trapped in the flour and your dough will stay together very easily.

Lasagne al Forno
Basic lasagne

At last, here is a basic recipe for assembling a lasagne, allowing you to combine ingredients and sauces of your choice, as well as to make the quantity of your choice. Of all baked pasta, the most famous is lasagne. Along with the classic spaghetti with tomato sauce, lasagne is probably the Italian dish which is the most popular and welcome on the dinner table. A versatile dish to make, lasagne can be made in advance or in stages. There are several versions of lasagne. Apart from the sauces used, what one needs to know is the method of assembling lasagne. When the method of assembly is clear, several recipes can be done easily, just changing the sauces.

The main components are sheets of lasagne, ragu' or other sauce (see page 53), Besciamella sauce (see page 47) and freshly grated Parmesan cheese. Fresh or dried pasta can be used, and in both cases the lasagne sheets should be boiled for about 2 minutes, if fresh, and 5–6 minutes, if dried, cooled in a bowl of cold water and placed on a clean tea towel to drain.

Apply a thin layer of Besciamella on the bottom of the ovenproof dish. Then alternate pasta sheets and ragu, pasta sheets and Besciamella, and maintain this sequence until the dish is full to the rim or until all the ingredients are used up. You might use up to seven layers of lasagne sheets. Make the last sauce on the top Besciamella, which keeps the dish really moist. Sprinkle grated Parmesan cheese onto each layer of sauce.

Preheat the oven to 180°C/350°F/Gas 4. Bake the lasagne for about 30 minutes, or until the top has a golden, bubbling crust. When the pasta is done, leave it to rest for a good 15 minutes. This will make it more compact and easier to serve.

Serving size optional

1 quantity Besciamella sauce (see page 47)

sheets of fresh or dried lasagne

1 quantity Ragu sauce (see page 53)

Parmesan cheese, as needed

My Secrets

Do not use too much sauce between the layers of pasta. A thin layer of each is enough to achieve the best results. I have been served lasagne which was drowning in Bolognese sauce, which is not the authentic Italian way.

The perfect lasagne should be served almost like a cake, and it should retain its shape.

Sauces

Sauces for pasta

Try some of these exquisite sauces from my family kitchen and you will be delighted with the results. There are suggestions for which types of pasta should be married with which sauce. Allow about 500 g/1 lb dried pasta to serve 4–6 people. The basic method for this is to bring salted water to a boil in a large saucepan, add the pasta, cook until al dente and drain.

Although there are hundreds of shapes and names of pasta, they can all be classified as long or short, flat or tubular, smooth or ridged. The question of which shape to put with what sauce is not too difficult to answer. A long, thin pasta, such as tagliolini, is perfect with a runny, smooth sauce that will not overpower its delicate shape. Tomato sauce or even a flavoured olive oil is ideal with spaghetti. A thick, chunky shape, such as large maccheroni, is happiest when matched with a strong, tasty sauce made with meat or sausage, or another ingredient of strong personality. The recipes I have selected for this book are good examples of what goes well together.

Don't drown the pasta in a sea of sauce. Some chefs who are trying to cook Italian tend to cover the pasta completely with sauce and cheese. Perhaps this is a convenient way to hide the poor quality of the pasta. The correct method is to add just enough sauce to lightly cover the pasta and no extra sauce should be found in the bottom of the bowl.

Salsa di Pomodoro a Modo Mio

Tomato sauce with all my secrets

Of all Italian dishes, this is the one with the most variations: everybody has their own 'best recipe'. Mine takes into account the fact that outside Italy, canned tomatoes are not always as good as they should be, and fresh tomatoes are often lacking in flavour. This versatile sauce also makes a good accompaniment to Corona di Riso (Crown of rice), see page 61.

Place the onion, carrot, celery and garlic in a saucepan with the olive oil and cook over a medium heat for about 5 minutes, until the onion is transparent but not brown.

Add the tomatoes and herbs, season with salt and pepper and simmer for 20–30 minutes, stirring occasionally.

Now, you could pass the sauce through a mouli-légumes to get a smoother texture, or you might use it as it is. If the sauce is made with fresh tomatoes, sieving will be necessary to get rid of the tomato skin and the pips.

Toss the tomato sauce with cooked pasta before serving.

Serves 4

½ small onion, very finely chopped

1 small carrot, very finely chopped

½ small stalk celery, very finely chopped

1 clove garlic, very finely chopped

4 tbsp olive oil

1 x 500 g/1 lb can tomatoes, or 1 kg/2 lb/ 5 cups fresh tomatoes, quartered

1 tbsp parsley, chopped

2–3 basil leaves

salt and pepper

My Secret
The flavours used to enhance the taste and the texture of a tomato sauce are, in most Italian recipes, celery, onion, carrot, garlic, parsley and basil. In my view, the only fat that can be used to make a perfect tomato sauce is olive oil.

Salsa ai Piselli

Pea sauce

Serves 6

500 g/1 lb/2½ cups petits pois or spring peas, fresh or frozen

5 tbsp single (light) cream

4–5 tbsp Parmesan cheese, grated

20, or more, basil leaves

1 tsp sugar

4 tbsp extra virgin olive oil

salt and freshly ground black pepper

This sauce, which could be called 'pea pesto', is ideal for short pasta such as smooth penne or maccheroni. The recipe was given to me by my niece, Francesca, who found it in a restaurant in Venice.

In a deep saucepan, cook the peas in boiling salted water until tender. Drain all but one-third of the peas, which should be reserved in the water.

Put the drained peas in a blender with the cream, Parmesan cheese, all but a few of the basil leaves, and the sugar. Process, adding the olive oil in a slow drizzle as if you were making mayonnaise. Stop adding the oil when the consistency of the sauce is like double cream. Season to taste.

To serve, dress cooked pasta with the sauce as soon as it is drained, decorating the plates with the reserved whole peas and the remaining basil leaves. Serve immediately sprinkled with freshly ground pepper.

My Secret

This sauce is quite thick and sticky, so it needs diluting with some water from the pasta pot. Do not be afraid of using up to a ladle of water when dressing the pasta to achieve good results.

Salsa di Pomodoro e Capperi di Renata

Sun-dried tomato and caper sauce

My Sicilian friend Renata gave me this recipe. It is very simple indeed, but has some very special ingredients that are delicious and make it ideal for summer. The sauce goes well with short pasta such as penne or rigatoni. Serve with plenty of Parmesan cheese, freshly grated, and a garnish of fresh basil.

In a large saucepan, sauté the onion and garlic gently in the oil until the onion is transparent but not brown.

Add the sun-dried tomatoes, olives and capers and cook for a few minutes, stirring gently.

Pour in the tomato passata, then add the chilli and basil and cook the sauce for 15 minutes over a medium heat.

Meanwhile, in a large saucepan, bring some salted water to a boil and cook the pasta until al dente.

Taste the sauce and add salt as necessary. To serve, dress cooked pasta with the sauce and sprinkle with the freshly grated Parmesan cheese. Garnish with some extra basil.

Serves 6

1 medium onion, chopped

2 cloves garlic, chopped

4 tbsp olive oil

6 oil-packed sun-dried tomato fillets, cut into strips

175 g/6 oz/¾ cup black olives, pitted and chopped

2 tbsp salt-preserved capers, rinsed

500 ml/1 pint/2½ cups passata, or sieved tomato

1 tsp dried chilli, crushed

12 basil leaves, plus extra to garnish

salt

3 tbsp Parmesan cheese, grated

My Secrets

Sun-dried tomatoes will provide a different taste and texture to fresh tomatoes. Their intense and concentrated flavour means that they should be used sparingly as an ingredient in Italian cooking, for specific dishes. They are best bought preserved in olive oil as dried ones will need to be soaked in water and placed in oil anyway, but resulting in a more chewy version.

Be careful when adding the salt to this dish. As the capers (even with rinsing) are very salty, no further additions may be needed.

Salsa al Gorgonzola

Gorgonzola cheese sauce

Serves 4–6

240 g/8 oz/1½ cups
gorgonzola cheese

120 g/4 oz/½ cup butter

150 ml/5 floz/½-⅔ cup
single (light) cream

a pinch of ground nutmeg

salt and pepper

3 tbsp Parmesan cheese,
grated

Very simple to prepare and yet delicious, the quality of this sauce (as with most Italian recipes) depends mostly on the quality of the ingredients used. When you buy the gorgonzola look for a very creamy variety. If you cannot find gorgonzola, Cambazola or Dolcelatte will do. This sauce is best used to dress short pasta such as conchiglie and penne, or gnocchi (potato dumplings).

Cut the cheese into chunks and place it in a saucepan with the butter over a very low heat. Gently cook the cheese, stirring occasionally, so that it melts without frying.

When the cheese is completely melted, add enough cream to give the sauce the consistency of custard – the amount of cream required will depend on the cheese used.

Add the nutmeg. Season the sauce with salt and pepper to taste, being careful not to add too much salt as the cheese is rather salty. To serve, dress the just-drained pasta with the sauce, then sprinkle with freshly grated Parmesan cheese.

My Secret
A pinch of grated nutmeg is perfect with all cheese-based sauces.

Besciamella

Béchamel sauce

This is one of the easiest and yet most difficult sauces. It has a French origin but it is widely used in Italian cooking and as it is part of several recipes in this book, it deserves very special attention. While there are many ways of making this sauce, the following method and quantities always work, and do not require a Cordon Bleu diploma for success.

In a saucepan, melt the butter over a medium heat. Stir in the flour with a wooden spoon to make a roux. Meanwhile, bring the milk to the boil (3 minutes at maximum power in the microwave oven will do the job).

Lower the heat and add the milk to the roux a little at a time, stirring constantly. Do not add any more milk until the previous addition has been well incorporated. Keep adding and stirring until all the milk is absorbed.

Season with nutmeg, salt and pepper and simmer, stirring from time to time, for a good 10 minutes. Your sauce is now ready to use.

For 500 ml/1 pint/2½ cups of sauce

4 tbsp butter

4 tbsp plain (all-purpose) white flour

500 ml/1 pint/2½ cups whole milk

½ tsp nutmeg, grated

salt and pepper

My Secrets

To make a good Besciamella, you need patience and a heavy base pan. Milk and flour easily stick to the bottom. A heavy pan on low heat (which means longer stirring) will guarantee success.

The quantities given here are a guideline but you don't really need to measure the ingredients, just take the same weight of flour and butter and add milk until you get the right thickness.

Besciamella thickens as it cools. Do not judge its consistency by the way it looks as soon as it is done. It will always look more liquid when hot than when it cools down.

Ragu' Vegetariano

Vegetarian ragu' sauce

Serves 4–6

5 tbsp olive oil

1 large onion, diced

2 cloves garlic, chopped

2 large carrots, diced

2 sticks celery, diced

2 courgettes (zucchini), diced

1 red or yellow bell pepper, cored and diced

300 g/10 oz/1½ cups chestnut mushrooms, diced

500 ml/1 pint/2½ cups canned chopped or plum Italian tomatoes

6–8 fresh basil leaves

salt and pepper

The word Ragu' originally meant 'stew', and in Italian cookery refers to a sauce for pasta made with meat. This is a vegetarian version of the classic meat Ragu', much lighter than the original, and ideal for lasagne, canelloni, tagliatelle, maccheroni and penne. I have put this together by mixing and matching recipes with vegetables and find this combination very successful.

In a large frying pan, heat the oil and sauté the onion and garlic over a high heat for a few minutes. Add the carrots and celery and continue cooking, tossing occasionally, for about 5 minutes or until the vegetables are golden.

Add the courgettes (zucchini) and bell pepper, and continue cooking and tossing over a high heat. Add the mushrooms and cook for about 5 minutes.

Add the tomatoes and basil to the pan and turn the heat down to medium. Simmer until the sauce gets rather thick but the vegetables are still crunchy. Season with salt and pepper.

Use the sauce for baked dishes as required or, if serving immediately with pasta, while the sauce is simmering, cook the pasta. Drain, then dress with the sauce.

My Secrets

All the vegetables should be cut quite evenly and small. The easiest way to do it is to use a long knife. Cut them into strips, and then holding them in a bunch, cut into dice.

The vegetables have different textures and cooking times, so it is important that they are not cooked all together. Do not add the rest of the vegetables until the onion, carrot and celery are golden.

You will notice that if the pan is crowded with vegetables you can leave the heat very high with no risk of burning.

Salsa al Tonno

Tuna fish sauce

My mother was always cooking this sauce on Fridays when, as a Catholic family, we couldn't eat meat. It was convenient for her to cook because the tuna is canned and she therefore did not have to go to the fishmonger. It is a very tasty and rather rustic sauce, very good for an informal party and ideal with linguine.

Heat the oil in a large pan and sauté the onion until clear and soft. Add the tomatoes and drained tuna and sauté over a medium heat for 15 minutes.

Lower the heat under the pan and cook, stirring well, for another 15 minutes. Season to taste.

To serve, toss the tuna sauce with cooked pasta and sprinkle with chopped parsley.

Serves 4–6

3 tbsp olive oil

1 large onion, thinly sliced

1 x 250 g/9 oz can plum or chopped tomatoes

1 x 240 g/8 oz can tuna fish in oil (not Skipjack, see page 73), drained

salt and pepper

1 tbsp parsley, chopped

My Secrets

Every time you sauté onions, sprinkle a little salt on them. It will cause them to release their juices, and it will be easier to cook them without burning.

Parsley is always welcome with fish. A little fresh parsley sprinkled on top of your pasta will give a perfect finish to any fish sauce.

Salsa di Cozze

Marinara sauce

Serves 4–6

1 kg/2¼ lb/2½ cups
mussels, unshelled

4 tbsp extra virgin olive oil

3 cloves garlic, sliced

1 tbsp parsley, chopped

1 tsp crushed dried chilli

Marinara sauce can be made with mussels or clams and should be accompanied by spaghetti. When I go to Riccione, I visit Fino's Restaurant by the harbour. Their recipe for this spaghetti is the best. They make it with clams, but mussels are more readily available in most supermarkets. Whether you choose mussels or clams, the method of cooking is the same. The shellfish should only be fresh and not frozen. The best way to enhance their flavour, as with most seafood, is to season them with garlic, fresh parsley, good olive oil and a touch of chilli. However, Parmesan cheese should never be used with seafood.

Wash each of the mussels under running water and pull off all of their the beards.

Put the mussels in a pot with no water in it and cover with the lid. Turn the heat to maximum. Every few minutes, holding the lid tight, shake the pot in order to move the mussels around. After about 10 minutes the shells should have opened. Discard those mussels that do not open or are broken.

Meanwhile, pick the mussels from their shells and reserve them. Reserve also a few spoonfuls of the juice at the bottom of the cooking pot to use when dressing the pasta.

In a saucepan, heat the oil, add the sliced garlic and fry over a medium heat for about 5 minutes, until it is golden. Add the mussels and stir quickly. Turn the heat off. Sprinkle the sauce with the parsley and chilli and dress your pasta.

My Secrets

Do not cook the mussels in the oil for more than 2 minutes, as they will become tough and rubbery.

Add some juice from the mussel pot to the pasta while dressing it to keep the pasta moist.

Salsa di Panna, Prosciutto e Piselli

Ham and pea sauce with cream

Here is a rather delicate sauce that goes well with a delicate pasta such as egg tagliatelle. It is similar to the well-known Alfredo sauce from the United States, but with the addition of the peas.

In a saucepan, melt the butter, add the chopped onion and sauté gently until the onion is golden. Add the diced ham and cook gently for about 5 minutes or until the ham starts to brown.

Add the frozen peas, 2 tablespoons of water, and simmer, covered, for 10-15 minutes until the peas are tender.

When the peas are cooked, stir in the cream and season the sauce with nutmeg, salt and pepper.

Dress cooked pasta with the sauce and sprinkle with freshly grated Parmesan cheese just before serving.

Serves 6

4 tbsp butter

1 small onion, chopped

90 g/3 oz/¼–½ cup Italian cooked ham, diced 0.5 cm/⅛ in thick

500 g/1 lb/2½ cups frozen petits pois or spring peas

150 ml/5 fl oz/½–⅔ cup single (light) cream

a pinch of nutmeg

salt and pepper

2 tbsp Parmesan cheese, grated

My Secrets

Unless you are sure that your peas are extremely fresh, use the frozen ones, which are always sweet and tender.

If you are unable to find Italian cooked ham, English honey roast ham is a good substitute.

Wait until the peas are cooked before seasoning them. This will keep them tender. Add some cooking water to the pasta while tossing.

Salsa di Pancetta e Zucchini

Courgette (zucchini) and pancetta sauce

Serves 4–6

4 courgettes (zucchini)

5 tbsp extra virgin olive oil

2 cloves garlic, sliced

90 g/3 oz/¼–½ smoked pancetta, diced

1 tsp dried Sicilian oregano

salt and pepper

3 tbsp Parmesan cheese, grated

This sauce is ideal with home-made egg pasta such as tagliolini or a dried pasta such as angel hair or fettuccine. Both shapes, being thin, are delicate and go well with courgettes (zucchini), which have a delicate taste.

Cut the courgettes (zucchini) lengthwise into sticks about 7.5 cm/3 in long, or a similar size to French fries.

In a frying pan, heat the olive oil and sliced garlic cloves until the garlic starts to colour. Add the courgette (zucchini) sticks and sauté over a high heat using 2 spatulas to toss them until the courgettes (zucchini) are golden but still al dente. Remove from the pan and reserve.

In the same pan, sauté the diced pancetta until golden but not too crisp. Return the courgettes (zucchini) to the pan and toss to combine. Add the dried Sicilian oregano (it is quite strong) and season with a little salt and pepper.

Dress cooked pasta with the courgette (zucchini) mixture. Sprinkle with Parmesan cheese and serve immediately.

My Secret

Egg pasta, fresh or dry, tends to become very dry when cooked and drained. It is essential to keep at least one ladle of cooking water to add to the pasta while dressing it. You'll be surprised to see that in a few minutes all the added water will have disappeared, leaving your dish really moist.

Ragu' Bolognese

Ragu' sauce

Ragu', often called bolognese outside Italy, is known all over the world and is a pillar of Italian cooking. Like many other famous recipes, it has been modified. Several brands of canned bolognese can be found on the market but they are different from what you would eat in Italy. Ragu' is ideal for lasagne, canelloni, tagliatelle, maccheroni and penne. During the BSE crisis I started making it with pork, chicken or lamb. Personally, I find that beef with a little minced pork is best. If you decide to use chicken, bear in mind that it is very lean, and you might have to use a little chopped pancetta to add some fat to the sauce. My aunt would turn in her grave if she saw me giving a recipe for ragu' with chicken mince. But she's my aunt, not yours!

Heat the butter or olive oil in a large pan and sauté the onions, carrots and celery until they are golden and the juices have evaporated.

Add the minced meat and mix it into the vegetables with a fork, making sure that there are no lumps of meat left. Cook over a high heat until the meat browns and all juices evaporate.

Add the tomatoes, bay leaves and season with salt and pepper. Cover and simmer for 2 hours on the lowest possible heat. Depending on how liquid the tinned tomatoes are, you might want to add some water or milk during cooking to prevent the sauce getting too dry.

Toss cooked pasta with the finished sauce. Always serve your ragu' pasta with grated Parmesan cheese.

Serves 6

4–5 tbsp melted butter or olive oil

2 medium onions, chopped

2 carrots, chopped

2 sticks celery, chopped

500 g/1 lb/2½ cups minced meat, such as beef, lamb, pork, or chicken

2 x 250 g/9 oz cans plum or chopped tomatoes

2 bay leaves

salt and pepper

2 tbsp Parmesan cheese, grated

My Secrets
The cooking time is the secret to make this sauce delicate and rich. Also, it is important to use a very heavy pan, such as cast iron or heavy terracotta, for best results. This will ensure even heating of the sauce.

Regardless of which type or types of meat you choose, it should ideally have a fat content of 10–20 percent.

To make the ragu' smoother, you can add some single (light) cream at the end if desired. Ragu' is inexpensive and freezes very well. I normally cook double the quantity given here and freeze half of it.

Salsa Amatriciana

Chilli and bacon sauce

Serves 6

1 small onion, chopped

4 tbsp butter

2 tbsp olive oil

210 g/7 oz/1 cup smoked pancetta, diced

1 x 250 g/9 oz can plum tomatoes

½ tsp crushed dried chilli

4 tbsp Parmesan cheese, grated

salt

The name of this sauce comes from a small village called Amatrice, near Rome. My first husband and I spent several holidays in Rome as guests of his mother. She had a cook, Paola, who cooked like an angel and looked like a barrel. I learned this recipe from her. It is a good example of how to match pasta and sauces: a delicate shape, such as fettuccine or angel hair wouldn't be right with amatriciana, which requires a strong, heavy shape of pasta. The best pasta shape for this sauce is bucatini, which are large spaghetti with a hole (buco in Italian) in the centre. If you can't find bucatini, use penne or maccheroni, short pastas, both of which are a good choice for guests who are not used to rolling spaghetti around a fork.

In a saucepan over a medium heat, sauté the onion in the butter and oil. When the onion is soft, add the diced pancetta and cook until the pancetta is golden but not crisp. Add the tomatoes and the chilli and salt and simmer for about 15 minutes.

To serve, toss the sauce with cooked pasta. The Parmesan cheese must be added by each person to their own taste at the table.

My Secrets

When adding the tomatoes to the pancetta, discard the juices from the tin as they will make the sauce too watery.

The true quantity of crushed chilli required depends on its quality and your taste. Personally, I prefer to use little, because if the sauce is too hot it overpowers the taste.

Salsina di Fegatini di Pollo

Chicken liver sauce

I learned how to cook chicken livers from my grandmother. When I was a child, I was put off by the sight of these small and bloody pieces of offal on the kitchen counter. I have since learned that they are a delicacy. This is a tasty sauce that goes best with a short pasta such as penne or maccheroni.

Marinate the chicken livers in the cognac overnight, or for several hours. When ready to cook, drain the livers and chop them roughly, discarding any white membranes.

Place half the butter in a frying pan and sweat the chopped spring onions. Add the livers and sauté over a high heat, tossing, until they are brown.

Pour in the white wine and let it evaporate. Lower the heat and simmer for 5 minutes to reduce the juices. Set aside.

Prepare the Besciamella sauce.

Pour the cooked Besciamella onto the mixture of liver and onions, season with salt and pepper and stir well. Dress cooked pasta with the sauce. Serve very hot with grated Parmesan cheese and chopped parsley.

Serves 4

500 g/1 lb/2½ cups chicken livers

4 tbsp cognac or brandy

4 tbsp butter

3 spring onions, chopped

4 tbsp white wine

250 ml/½ pint/1¼ cups Besciamella sauce (see page 47)

salt and pepper

4 tbsp Parmesan cheese, grated

1 tbsp parsley, chopped

My Secrets

Always check for bile sacs attached to the livers. Nowadays, livers are sold ready to be cooked, however, sometimes you might find a small green sac attached: that is the bile. It should be removed intact and discarded. If you notice that the sac is broken, discard all the livers as the bitterness of the bile will ruin the whole dish, and unfortunately, it cannot be washed away once the sac is broken.

Do not cook the livers for more than about 5 minutes as they will become rubbery.

Risotto

The essence of risotto

I didn't learn how to cook risotto until I married and spent some time in the kitchen with Giuditta, my husband's nanny.

Rice is grown in the northern part of Italy, along the Po Valley, where the land is marshy and the weather humid. The best risottos can be found in the area between Turin and Venice.

Cooking a perfect risotto is easy, but it requires practice. Once you've done it a couple of times, you'll be very confident and relaxed about it. Using a heavy based pot will help you cook the rice well without it sticking to the bottom. Stirring constantly with a wooden spoon also prevents sticking.

To ensure a perfect risotto, never rinse the rice before cooking. Rinsing would wash away some of the starch and the final dish would not be as creamy as it should be.

Always cook the risotto on the top of the stove, and add your preferred liquid (it can be vegetable, fish, or meat stock, depending on the recipe) a little at a time, while you keep stirring. This process allows the grains to release their starch and makes the risotto creamy, runny and delicate, while still al dente!

Always check the cooking time: never more than 16 minutes from the time the rice goes into the pot. I like to turn the heat off exactly 14 minutes after I have started and finish by adding the cheese and butter off the heat.

Never offer risotto to guests who make a habit of being late! Your risotto will become gluey and unappetising if served more than a few minutes after being cooked.

Risotto Giallo alla Milanese

Milanese saffron risotto

Originally, Risotto Giallo alla Milanese required a couple of spoonfuls of beef marrow mixed with the onions to add taste and fat to the risotto. This tradition has disappeared, as nowadays people are more health conscious and the final addition of butter to the rice gives it a rich taste anyway. I think this is one of the best risottos. It is perfect matched with Ossobuco alla Milanese (Ossobuco Milanese style), see page 76, or Brasato di Manzo al Vino Bianco (Beef stew with onions and white wine), see page 75, but can also be served on its own, as a starter.

Melt half the butter in a deep saucepan, then add the onion and sauté until it is translucent but not browned. Meanwhile, in a separate pan, put the stock on to boil.

Using a wooden spoon, stir the rice into the onion and continue sautéing for a couple of minutes, mixing gently until all the rice is coated with butter.

Add the wine and let the rice absorb it, then add just enough boiling stock to cover the rice and stir well. When the rice has absorbed all the liquid, add a little more stock and continue cooking, stirring constantly. Repeat with the rest of the stock, cooking the rice for 14 minutes and no more.

Turn off the heat and add the Parmesan cheese, saffron and the rest of the butter and stir well. Serve immediately.

Serves 6

120 g/4 oz/½ cup butter

1 small onion, finely chopped

1 litre/2 pints/5 cups chicken stock

500 g/1 lb/2½ cups arborio rice

250 ml/9 fl oz/1 cup dry white wine

4 tbsp Parmesan cheese, grated

⅓ tsp powdered saffron, or 1 tsp saffron strands

My Secrets

The rice keeps absorbing the stock even after it is removed from the heat. Make sure the risotto is more liquid than you think it should be, because by the time it goes from the pot to the table, it will have absorbed more stock and will be much drier than when you turned the heat off. In Milan, we say that a good risotto must be 'all' onda', which means 'wavy'.

The process of stirring the butter in at the end of cooking is called 'mantecare' from the Spanish word 'matequilla', which means butter. Mantecare is important because it makes the risotto creamy.

Risotto ai Funghi Porcini

Risotto with wild mushrooms

Serves 6

60 g/2 oz/4 level tbsp
dried wild mushrooms

120 g/4 oz/½ cup butter

1 small onion, chopped

1 litre/2 pints/5 cups
vegetable stock, made
with 3 Italian stock cubes

500 g/1 lb/2½ cups arborio
rice

120 ml/4 fl oz/½ cup dry
white wine

6 tbsp Parmesan cheese,
grated

Dried wild mushrooms lend to rice a very special, sophisticated taste that makes this an ideal dish for a dinner party.

Place the mushrooms in a small bowl, cover with about
300 ml/10 fl oz/1¼ cups of hot water and soak for at least 30 minutes.

In a deep, heavy pan, melt half the butter. Add the onion and sauté for a few minutes until it is transparent but not brown. Meanwhile, in a separate saucepan, bring the stock to a boil.

Lift the mushrooms from their soaking water and add them to the onion. Add the rice and stir carefully with a wooden spoon until the rice is thoroughly coated with butter.

Add the wine, allowing it to sizzle and be absorbed by the rice. Stir the mixture thoroughly.

Sieve the water in which the mushrooms were soaking through a muslin cloth or kitchen paper and add it to the boiling stock.

Over a medium heat, add just enough stock to cover the rice and stir continuously. When the rice has absorbed all the stock and starts to look dry again, add more stock to cover the rice.

Continue the process of stirring and adding stock for 14 minutes from the time the rice went into the pot. After this time, the rice should still be wet, like a thick soup. If you find it too dry, add some more stock and stir.

Turn the heat off and add the Parmesan cheese and the remaining butter. Stir well to blend the butter and cheese into the rice. Transfer to a serving dish and serve immediately.

My Secret
Whenever you have soaked dried mushrooms, remember to retain the liquid as it becomes an extremely flavoursome stock for use in risottos and soups.

Corona di Riso

Crown of rice

Risotto must be served immediately, it doesn't wait. In this dish, however, that rule does not apply and the rice can be prepared in advance. A crown of rice, filled with your favourite sauce, makes a very good first course for an important meal. I once served it as a starter when I invited my boss for dinner and it was a great success!

Butter a ring-shaped mould of 750 ml/1½ pints/3¼ cup capacity and set aside.

In a heavy saucepan, melt 4 tablespoons of the butter and sauté the onion until golden. Meanwhile, in a separate saucepan, bring the stock to a boil.

Add the rice to the onion and toss carefully until the grains are all coated with butter. Add the white wine and let it evaporate, stirring continuously over a medium heat.

Carefully add all the the boiling stock to the rice along with the saffron and continue stirring for 10–12 minutes.

Remove the saucepan from the heat and add the beaten eggs, Parmesan cheese the remaining butter and season with salt and pepper. Stir quickly to blend all the ingredients into the rice mixture.

Fill the buttered mould with the rice, pressing the it down gently.

Heat the oven to 180°C/350°F/Gas 4 and bake the rice for about 20 minutes to finish cooking. Set aside to rest for 15 minutes.

Turn the rice ring out onto a warmed serving dish and fill the centre with your favourite sauce – classic tomato sauce is ideal, see page 43. Sprinkle with Parmesan cheese and serve immediately.

Serves 8

6 tbsp butter

1 medium onion, chopped

1 litre/2 pints/5 cups stock, made with 2 Italian stock cubes

700 g/1½ lb/3½ cups arborio rice

180 ml/6 fl oz/¾ cup dry white wine

½ tsp powdered saffron or 1½ tsp saffron strands

2 eggs, beaten

salt and pepper

5–6 tbsp Parmesan cheese, grated plus extra to serve

My Secret

It is important to wait at least 15 minutes before unmoulding the rice ring. It is likely to break if it is turned out as soon as it is taken from the oven, or while still very hot.

Risotto agli Spinaci

Risotto with spinach

Serves 6

120 g/4 oz/½ cup butter

1 small onion, finely chopped

500 g/1lb frozen spinach, defrosted

1 litre/2 pints/5 cups meat stock

500 g/1 lb/2½ cups arborio rice

6 tbsp grated Parmesan cheese

salt and pepper

This is a favourite with my daughters – I used to cook it when they were small as it was a great way of getting them to eat a well-balanced meal, including vegetables, dairy products and grains. But it is just as good for a smart dinner party.

Melt the butter in a frying pan, add the onion and sauté it gently until translucent and lightly coloured.

In the meantime, squeeze the spinach very well to remove as much water as possible. Chop the spinach in a food processor until it is a paste. Add the spinach to the onions and stir well until the spinach is warmed. In the meantime, bring the stock to the boil in a separate saucepan.

Add the rice and stir well. Simmer for a couple of minutes. Add enough boiling stock to cover the rice and spinach. Stir and cook over a medium heat. Proceed in the usual way until the rice is cooked: about 14 minutes from the start of the cooking time.

Season with the grated Parmesan cheese, salt and pepper to taste and, if necessary, add a little extra stock to obtain a creamy texture.

My Secret
To obtain a very velvety and smooth texture, make sure the spinach is very finely chopped before adding it to the pan.

Risotto al Radicchio

Risotto with radicchio

Radicchio is a salad leaf typical of the Veneto region and is a member of the endive or chicory family. There are two kinds of radicchio: trevigiana, which has long leaves and a very distinguished taste, and the round cabbage-type one, from Chioggia. Like all endives, radicchio has a very subtle bitter aftertaste.

Heat the oil and half the butter together in a frying pan. Add the onion and radicchio and cook over a medium heat until the radicchio starts to wilt. Add the wine and simmer gently until the liquid has completely evaporated.

Add the rice and toss to mix all the ingredients together. In the meantime, bring the stock to the boil in a separate saucepan.

Cover the rice with boiling stock. Simmer, adding stock as the rice absorbs it. Proceed, using the same method for risotto with spinach as on page 62.

Turn the heat off after 14 minutes from the time the rice was added to the pan. Add the grated Parmesan cheese, season with salt and pepper add and the remaining butter. Stir, adding stock if necessary, to make the rice creamy. Serve immediately.

Serves 6

2 tbsp olive oil

120 g/4 oz/½ cup butter

1 small onion, finely chopped

500 g/1 lb radicchio, washed and shredded

100 ml/3 fl oz/1 cup dry white wine

500 g/1 lb/2½ cups arborio rice

1 litre/2 pints/5 cups meat stock

6 tbsp grated Parmesan cheese

salt and pepper

My Secret
The best season for radicchio is from November to March. Whenever possible, try to use ingredients in season for the best results.

Risotto al Basilico

Risotto with basil

Serves 6

120 g/4 oz/½ cup butter

1 small onion, finely chopped

1 litre/2 pints/5 cups meat stock

500 g/1 lb/2½ cups arborio rice

6 tbsp grated Parmesan cheese

salt and pepper

3 tbsp basil, chopped

This risotto is very easy to prepare, is very elegant and makes an ideal starter for a smart dinner party.

Melt the butter, add the onion and sautè it gently until translucent and lightly coloured. In a separate pan, bring the stock to the boil.

Add all the rice to the onions and stir well to coat with the butter. Simmer for a few minutes. Add enough boiling stock to cover the rice, then stir and cook over a medium heat.

Proceed, in the usual way, until the rice is cooked, for about 14 minutes from the beginning of the cooking time.

Season with the Parmesan cheese, salt and pepper to taste and, if necessary, add a little extra boiling stock to obtain a runny texture.

Add the chopped basil, stir well and serve immediately.

My Secret

Basil should not be washed, simply wiped gently with a cloth. If your basil plant has gone to seed, use the top with the flowers as well as the leaves as they have plenty of taste.

Basil releases all its flavour when added to a warm base – it should not be cooked. That is why it is added to the rice just before serving.

Risotto alle Ortiche

Risotto with nettles

Nettles are used as a green vegetable in many parts of Italy. The best season for them is spring, when the young shoots are tender and their taste is at its most delicate.

Wash the nettles well in cold water. Bring a large pan of water to the boil. Add salt, then plunge in the nettles. As soon as the water returns to the boil, turn it off and drain the nettles. You can now handle them as if they were any other vegetable, squeezing them to remove excess moisture.

Heat the oil and half the butter together in a frying pan. Add the onion and nettles and cook over a medium heat. Add the wine and simmer until the liquid has completely evaporated.

Add the rice and toss to mix all the ingredients together. In the meantime, bring the stock to the boil in a separate saucepan.

Cover the rice with boiling stock. Simmer, adding stock as the rice absorbs it. Proceed, using the same method for risotto with spinach as on page 62.

Turn the heat off after 14 minutes from the time the rice was added to the pan. Add the grated Parmesan cheese, season with salt and pepper. Stir, adding stock if necessary, to make the rice creamy. Serve immediately.

Serves 6

500 g/1 lb nettles

salt

2 tbsp olive oil

120 g/4 oz/½ cup butter

1 small onion, finely chopped

100 ml/3 fl oz/1 cup dry white wine

500 g/1 lb/2½ cups arborio rice

1 litre/2 pints/5 cups meat stock

6 tbsp grated Parmesan cheese

salt and pepper

My Secret

Always wear rubber gloves to pick nettles. They should always be blanched before using in order to destroy the formic acid that gives them their sting.

When picking nettles, pick only the top small leaves, never the large ones and the stalks, as they are tough and bitter.

Risotto alla Crema di Scampi

Risotto with prawns (shrimp), cream and brandy

Serves 4

For the stock:

1 litre/2 pints water

½ onion

1 celery stalk

1 small bunch parsley

1 bay leaf

100 ml/4 fl oz/½ cup dry white wine

salt

For the risotto:

330 g/11 oz/1½ cups arborio rice

the white part of 2 shallots, or 4 spring onions, finely chopped (minced)

30 g/1 oz/2 tbsp butter

1 tbsp olive oil

For the prawn cream:

500 g/1 lb uncooked prawns (shrimp) in their shells

45 g/1½ oz/3 tbsp butter

2 tbsp brandy

salt and pepper

2 tbsp whipping (light whipping) cream

1 tbsp parsley, chopped

I was introduced to this very delicate dish several years ago in a small family restaurant in Venice. Although it is slightly more elaborate than the usual method for risotto, it is well worth the effort.

First, prepare the stock with all the ingredients except the wine. Bring to the boil, then cook for 15 minutes.

Add the wine and the uncooked prawns (shrimp) and cook for 5 minutes. Remove the prawns from the stock and shell them, reserving the shells.

Return the shells to the stock and simmer for about 30 minutes to give extra flavour to the stock. This completes the first stage, which can be done in advance. Once the vegetables and shells are discarded, and the stock is sieved, you should end up with about 600 ml/1 pint of stock ready for use.

In a large frying pan, quickly sauté the shelled prawns (shrimp) in the butter. When sizzling, splash with the brandy and season to taste. Let the brandy evaporate and reduce. Add the cream and turn the heat off.

Blend half of this mixture into a cream-like texture in a food processor and reserve the remainder.

Sieve the stock to remove the vegetables and prawn (shrimp) shells.

To make the risotto, gently sweat the shallots in a heavy pan in the butter and oil. When the shallots look soft and transparent, add the rice all in one go. Stir well, then begin to add the boiling stock, one ladle at a time, as it is absorbed.

Keep adding stock to maintain a thick, creamy consistency. After 12–13 minutes, add the cream of prawns and the whole creamy prawns. Stir briefly, turn the heat off. Check the seasoning and adjust if necessary.

Transfer to the serving dish, garnish with the chopped parsley and serve.

My Secret

Depending on how much stock you have (it may have reduced a little while cooking), your risotto could be a little too dry when cooked and ready to serve. If so, just add a little boiling water and stir – you'll have the perfect texture.

Risotto all' Aragosta al Profumo di Limone

Risotto with lobster and lemons

This risotto is quite delicious and will make a terrific impression on your guests. It is not particularly difficult to prepare – the only somewhat challenging part is boiling the lobster and shelling it. The method is very similar to the previous recipe.

Prepare the stock as for the risotto with prawns (shrimp), cream and brandy recipe on page 66. You will need more than ½ litre/1 pint water to submerge the lobster, but only ½ litre/1 pint stock.

When the stock is boiling, plunge the lobster into it and cook for about 5 minutes, until the shell turns bright red. With tongs, transfer the lobster to a colander to cool.

When it is cool enough to handle, cut the lobster in half lengthways with a large knife and remove the meat from the tail. Extract meat from the claws by breaking the shells with a rolling pin. Cut the lobster meat into small cubes and return the shell to the stock to simmer, while you start the risotto.

In a heavy pan, melt the butter and gently cook the onions until soft but not coloured. Add the rice and cook it on a high heat for a few minutes.

Meanwhile, sieve the stock (you do not want to add lobster shells to the rice!). Add one or two ladles of boiling stock and stir while simmering. Keep the risotto wet by adding more stock as it is absorbed. After about 10 minutes, add the lobster meat to the rice. Stir and continue cooking the rice for another 4–5 minutes.

Turn the heat off and season to taste with salt and pepper. Add the rind of the lemon and the lemon juice. Stir again, garnish with chopped parsley and serve.

Serves 4

For the stock:

½ litre/1 pint/2½ cups water

½ onion

1 celery stalk

1 small bunch parsley

1 bay leaf

100 ml/4 fl oz/½ cup dry white wine

salt

For the risotto:

1 lobster, weighing at least 500 g/1 lb

60 g/3 oz/½ cup butter

the white part of 2 shallots, or 4 spring onions, finely chopped

330 g/11 oz/1½ cups arborio rice

salt and pepper to taste

rind of 1 lemon, grated

juice of 1 lemon

parsley, chopped, to garnish

My Secret

If you do this recipe in two stages, you'll find it a lot easier. First, boil the lobster, shell it and finish cooking the stock with all the bits in it, then sieve the stock. You can keep the lobster and the stock in the fridge, then reheat the stock when you are ready to prepare the rice.

Roasts and Sautés

Cooking poultry, meat and fish

Traditionally, Italian cooking doesn't have many recipes that call for oven roasting. Until the 1920s and 30s, kitchens in Italy were equipped with charcoal or wood-fired stoves. The stove provided surface heat for cooking and space heating for the home. Traditional ovens were seldom found and this is why, in Italian cookery, pot-roasting on top of the stove is more common.

This method is excellent because it keeps the meat pleasingly moist and it is very easy to control. If you wish to roast your meat in the oven, please do so, but only after the first stage of sealing and browning the meat on top of the stove.

The pot-roasts in this chapter have the same method in common. The ingredients change, and the outcomes are very different, but the cooking steps are the same. My mother always started a roast with oil and butter mixed together: the oil can reach high temperatures before burning, but it won't colour the meat. Butter will give a nice golden colour, but will burn if brought to a high temperature. By mixing the two, you get the best of both. Another pot-roast secret is to make sure the thickness of the juices in the pot is runny but not too liquid, at the end of cooking.

Sautéing is another popular method for cooking meat and fish. It is simple and straightforward. On occasions, you will find that your ingredients vary in texture, tenderness, or moistness from day to day. For example, a particular veal escalope can release a lot of juice while cooking, while another one can cook nicely and retain all the moisture. Helping you to understand how to handle that ingredient that behaves differently while still achieving the best results is my ambition. Once you understand the techniques you can stop paying attention to the 'step-by-step' aspect of a recipe, begin to relax in your kitchen and enjoy cooking.

Branzino al Cartoccio con le Olive

Sea bass surprise

Amongst Mediterranean fish, sea bass is one of the nicest and most elegant. Best results are achieved when the bass is a fairly large one, because the flesh stays moist and juicy, which is more difficult to achieve with a smaller fish. Serve this dish on a very special occasion, accompanied by a simple side salad.

Heat the oven to 180°C/350°F/Gas 4. Take an ovenproof dish or baking tray big enough to contain the whole fish. Cut a large sheet of parchment paper or foil that will wrap the fish easily, but allow some air to circulate inside the parcel. Place the paper on the dish and lay a bed of onion rings on the paper. Lay the fish on the onion rings.

Add the tomatoes, olives, capers, oregano, parsley, garlic and some salt and pepper, placing some around the fish, some on top, and some in the cavity. Drizzle the oil on top.

Seal the parcel carefully and bake for 40 minutes. Turn the oven off and leave the fish in the oven for 15 minutes. Bring the wrapped fish to the table and open the parcel in front of your guests so that they can enjoy the aromas when released.

Serves 4

1 sea bass, about
1.8 kg/4 lb, gutted and
scaled

1 red onion, sliced into
rings

100 g/3½ oz/½ cup canned
plum tomatoes, drained

12 black olives

3 tbsp salt-preserved
capers, rinsed

2 tsp parsley, chopped

2 tsp dried oregano

2 cloves garlic, peeled and
halved

salt and pepper

3 tbsp extra virgin olive oil

My Secrets

The paper shields the fish from direct heat, so it is advisable to leave the fish in the oven for 15 minutes after it has been turned off to ensure that the fish is cooked to perfection without being overdone.

The bass is cooked perfectly when the meat comes off the bone easily. You can have a quick look in the parcel to check that it is done, if you like.

Pesce Spada ai Capperi

Swordfish with capers

Serves 6

2 tbsp salt-preserved
capers, rinsed

2–3 cloves garlic

2 tbsp parsley, chopped

1 tbsp rosemary, chopped

1 tbsp marjoram, chopped

juice of 1 lemon

3 tbsp olive oil

6 swordfish steaks, about
1 cm/½ in thick

2 lemons, sliced

salt and pepper

Swordfish is very popular in Sicily. It is one of my favourite fish, not only because it is delicious, but also because it brings back wonderful memories of summer holidays spent in Sicily. One of the ingredients we use in this recipe is capers. Capers (the buds of the caper flower) grow wild on the Sicilian islands and in that area are preserved in coarse salt. This is a much better way to preserve them than in vinegar, which spoils the taste of the capers.--

Preheat the oven to 190°C/375°F/Gas 5.

Chop the capers and garlic together with all the herbs. Stir in the lemon juice and olive oil.

Coat each swordfish steak with the mixture and place in a dish. Pour any remaining mixture over the top and leave to marinate for 2 hours.

Arrange a bed of lemon slices in an ovenproof dish and lay the steaks on top and season with salt and pepper. Bake for 10 minutes and serve hot with a potato salad, if you like.

My Secrets

If you are not sure that the fish is done, turn the oven off and leave the fish in with the door slightly open. Those few extra minutes in the oven will make sure that the fish is done but not overcooked.

As an alternative method, try cooking this wonderful fish wrapped in foil on the barbecue.

Tonno alla Siciliana

Sicilian-style tuna

This dish is very easy to prepare. As with any fish recipe, the freshness of the main ingredient is vital.

Pierce the tuna loin about 10 times all over with a thin, sharp knife. Insert a mint leaf, coated with salt and pepper, into each cut. Lightly coat the tuna with flour.

In a casserole, heat the oil and fry the tuna over a high heat to colour it on all sides. (The purpose of this step is to colour the tuna, not to finish cooking it.) When the tuna is golden all over, remove it from the casserole.

In the same casserole, gently fry the onions and garlic in the remaining oil, until soft. Replace the tuna, add the tomato sauce and simmer gently for 5–10 minutes. Add a large glass of water, cover with a lid and cook for a further 20 minutes.

To serve, slice the tuna and arrange it on a serving dish, with the sauce poured over. Garnish with parsley and serve with crusty bread and a side salad.

Serves 6–8

1 kg/2¼ lb tuna loin, in one piece

10 small mint leaves

salt and pepper

3 tbsp plain (all-purpose) white flour

4 tbsp olive oil

2 medium onions, sliced

1 clove garlic, chopped

1 litre/2 pints/4½ cups passata or sieved tomatoes

1 tbsp parsley, chopped, to garnish

My Secret
Sometimes tuna can be very bloody, so rinse it under running water and pat dry with kitchen paper (paper towels) to remove excess blood and juices. It will then be easier to fry, as well.

roasts and sautés **73**

Agnello al Forno

Roast lamb

Serves 5–6

5 tbsp olive oil

juice of 1 large lemon

3 sprigs rosemary, chopped

4 leaves sage, chopped

3 sprigs thyme, chopped

1 tsp salt

1 tsp pepper

1 leg lamb, about 2.5 kg/5 lb, boned and trimmed of all fat

5–6 cloves garlic

This dish is from my ex-mother-in-law. She is not a great cook (not all Italians are), but with this lamb she was unsurpassed. The recipe is very simple and somewhat different from that which the British palate is used to. In Italy, lamb is not as popular as in the United Kingdom. But it is the typical Easter meal, served with baked potatoes. Italian joints of lamb are always much smaller than in the United Kingdom, as lambs are slaughtered when still milk fed. This is why it is mainly served for Easter, in spring.

Combine the olive oil, lemon juice, rosemary, sage, thyme, salt and pepper to make a marinade. Using a small, sharp knife, pierce the meat several times and insert a garlic clove in each hole. Place in a container and turn the meat several times to ensure it is covered with marinade.

Cover with plastic wrap or foil and marinate in the fridge overnight.

Preheat the oven to 200°C/400°F/Gas 6. Place the meat in a roasting tin and cook for about 30 minutes to seal.

Lower the oven temperature to 180°C/350°F/Gas 4 and cook for another 50–60 minutes, basting occasionally, until the outside is brown but the meat is still juicy. It should be well done and tender, but not pink.

When cooked, carve the meat and serve it on a warmed serving dish with the pan juices.

My Secret
The meat should be almost overcooked, as if it were coming off the bone (though there is no bone). If you notice that the outer surface of the joint is getting a bit dry, cover it with foil to allow the meat to cook well, without the outside becoming crisp.

Brasato di Manzo al Vino Bianco

Beef stew with onions and white wine

Brasato al Barolo is a classic of Piedmontese cooking. This is a revised version that I first tasted at the restaurant 'la Scaletta' in Milan. Using white wine instead of red gives a lighter taste. For best results, choose a lean piece of beef such as silverside.

In a dish, marinate the whole joint of meat overnight with the wine, the roughly cut vegetables and garlic.

Heat the butter and oil in a casserole dish that will contain the meat snugly. Drain the meat, reserving the wine and vegetables separately, and place it in the casserole. Brown it on all sides over a very high heat – do not pierce the meat when turning it.

Add the drained vegetables and cook until they are starting to brown and release some moisture. Then add the wine from the marinade, the bay leaves and the cloves. Lower the heat and simmer, covered, for about 1½ hours.

Remove the meat from the casserole dish and set aside in a warm place. Purée the vegetables and cooking juices in a blender or mouli-légumes – if the result is too liquid you can reduce the sauce by simmering it for a few minutes uncovered.

Slice the meat very thinly and lay it in a warm serving dish with the slices overlapping. Pour the sauce over the meat and serve with risotto or mashed potatoes, see page 110.

Serve 6

1½ kg/3 lb silverside beef

300 ml/10 fl oz/1¼ cups dry white wine

2 onions, roughly chopped

2 carrots, roughly chopped

2 sticks celery, roughly chopped

2 cloves garlic

4 tbsp butter

3 tbsp olive oil

4 bay leaves

3 cloves

salt and pepper, to taste

My Secrets

Slicing the meat very thinly (about 0.6 cm/¼ in thick) is difficult while it is warm. Let the meat cool before slicing. You'll be surprised how easy it is!

Once sliced, cover with the blended sauce and reheat it in the oven. Do not leave the meat uncovered by the sauce, as it tends to dry out.

Ossobuco alla Milanese

Ossobuco Milanese style

Serves 4

4 ossobuchi

2 tbsp olive oil

plain (all-purpose) white flour, for coating

4 tbsp butter

1 small onion, chopped

½ stick celery, chopped

150 ml/5 fl oz/⅔ cup dry white wine

300 ml/10 fl oz/1¼ cups stock, made with stock cubes

1 tbsp parsley, chopped

½ clove garlic

finely grated zest of 1 lemon

salt and pepper

In Italian, ossobuco *means 'bone with a hole'. There are basically two versions of the ossobuco recipe: one made with tomato sauce and the other with white wine. Personally, I prefer the latter as it is more delicate. The best and only meat to use for this recipe is veal; the part of the animal is the lower leg. Its quality is essential to the outcome: the ossobuco must be cut properly and the* buco *(the hole) must have plenty of marrow. The ideal accompaniment is the classic* Risotto Giallo alla Milanese *(Milanese saffron Risotto), see page 58.*

Choose a frying pan large enough to fit all the ossobuchi in one layer. Heat the oil. Lightly coat the ossobuchi with flour then brown them in the oil on both sides. Remove them from the pan and reserve.

Add the butter, chopped onion and celery and a pinch of salt and pepper to the pan. Cook gently over a low heat. When the vegetables are soft, return the meat to the pan and cover with the wine. Simmer until the liquid is almost completely evaporated.

Pour the hot stock over the ossobuchi, lower the heat and cover with a tight-fitting lid. Cook gently for 1½ hours, turning every 20 minutes or so, until the meat is almost coming off the bone.

Transfer the ossobuchi to a serving dish and keep warm. To finish the sauce, make a gremolata by chopping the parsley and garlic very finely and adding them to the pan with the finely grated lemon zest. Stir to combine, then pour over the ossobuchi before serving.

My Secret

Ask your butcher to cut the *ossobuchi* about 2.5 cm/1 in thick.

When turning the ossibuchi, make sure that you lift them gently using one or two spatulas so that they stay in one piece and the marrow is not lost.

Il Polpettone della Giudi

My nanny's meatloaf

Meatloaf may sound rather ordinary, but this one is excellent and can, in my opinion, be served at a dinner party or buffet. Serve it warm, as a pot roast, with some petits pois, or cold, in summer with some mayonnaise and a mixed salad.

In a large bowl, mix together the minced (ground) meat, mortadella, Parmesan cheese and parsley. Add the raw eggs to bind the ingredients.

Tear the bread into small pieces and place in a small saucepan with just enough milk to wet the bread. Heat gently, stirring until all the bread is mashed. Add the bread to the other ingredients and season with salt and pepper. Mix everything, first with a fork and then with your hand.

Place the mixture on a large sheet of parchment paper and shape it into a very large sausage about 7.5 cm/3 in diameter. Insert the hard-boiled eggs into the sausage, making sure they are centred in the loaf. Coat the loaf with flour and wrap it in the paper, tying with some kitchen string.

Heat the butter and oil in a large pan. Lay the wrapped loaf in the pan and cook for 8–10 minutes, turning so that all sides are heated. Be careful not to pierce the paper.

When the oil and butter start to smoke, pour in the white wine and add the herbs. Cover and cook for about 1 hour, still wrapped in paper. Add some water to keep the bottom of the pot moist if necessary.

After 1 hour, unwrap the meatloaf and return it to the pan for a few minutes to coat it with the gravy. Place on a warmed dish and serve immediately.

Serves 6

600 g/1 lb 3 oz/3 cups minced (ground) beef, pork or veal

4–5 slices mortadella, chopped

4–5 tbsp Parmesan cheese, grated

2 tbsp parsley, chopped

2 raw eggs, plus 2–3 hard-boiled eggs, peeled

2 slices white bread

milk, for soaking

salt and pepper

plain (all-purpose) white flour, for coating

4 tbsp butter

3 tbsp olive oil

180 ml/6 fl oz/¾ cup white wine

1 sprig rosemary

2–3 sage leaves

My Secrets

If you can't find any mortadella, use a cooked ham instead, choosing a fatty quality, which will make the loaf moist.

To check that the meat is cooked, use a spatula to press gently on the meat. If it is cooked, it should feel firm and compact.

If you have a hard time slicing the meat, let it cool first.

Le Mie Polpettine di Carne

My meatballs

Serves 6

2 slices white bread

6 tbsp milk

90 g/3 oz/¼–½ cup mortadella

½ tsp parsley, chopped

500 g/1 lb/2½ cups lean minced (ground) meat, beef or pork

4–5 tbsp Parmesan cheese, grated

1 large egg

salt and pepper

plain (all-purpose) white flour, for coating

4 tbsp butter

4 tbsp olive oil

150 ml/5 fl oz/½-⅔ cup white wine

My mother always said that I shouldn't choose meatballs when going to a restaurant because they would be made with second-grade ingredients. She was very fussy (and I am, too). It is true that to achieve the best results, one must use the best ingredients. But try my meatballs, and you will be convinced that they can be served even to a fussy guest.

Soak the bread in the milk until soft. Mash it with a fork, then place in a small saucepan and cook over a very low heat for a few minutes until the bread comes apart.

In a food processor, chop the mortadella and parsley. Transfer to a large bowl and mix in the minced (ground) meat, bread, Parmesan cheese and egg. Season with salt and pepper, and mix with your hands until well blended.

Shape the mixture into balls the size of an apricot and coat them lightly with plain flour.

Heat the butter and olive oil in a large frying pan. Working in batches if necessary, add the meatballs to the pan in one layer and brown them on all sides, turning gently with two forks and taking care not to pierce them. There is no need to add any extra fat to the pan for the subsequent batches.

When all the meatballs have been cooked, return them to the pan as necessary over a high heat and splash them with the wine while moving them around – the wine will blend with the meat juices and flour, making a delicious, glossy gravy.

My Secrets

While shaping the meatballs, wet your hands: the mixture will not stick to your hands, and it will be easier to roll them.

Meatballs can be made in advance, frozen and reheated without harm.

As an alternative to the wine gravy, add some tomato sauce and simmer for a few minutes, before adding some fresh basil.

If you want to serve them as we do in Italy, a perfect accompaniment is mashed potatoes. Spaghetti with meatballs is a heresy, used only by Americans, and only found in restaurants for tourists in Italy!

Arrosto di Maiale al Latte

Pork loin with milk sauce

Combining milk and pork might sound unusual, yet it is very popular in Italian cookery. You will be surprised how tender and delicate the meat becomes. It's an excellent choice for a special occasion. Accompany with spinach, boiled potatoes or rice.

Choose a heavy-based pot not much larger than the piece of meat. Trim the pork thoroughly of all visible fat.

Heat the oil and butter in the pot, then add the meat. Cook it over a high heat, turning, until sealed and golden on all sides. Add the vegetables to the pot and cook for 3–5 minutes, stirring constantly to prevent sticking.

When the vegetables have released their moisture and are almost starting to burn, add some of the milk, the herbs, nutmeg, and salt and pepper. Turn the contents of the pot again and then add enough milk to cover the meat.

Simmer for about 1½ hours, turning the meat from time to time and being careful that the milk doesn't boil over.

When the meat is cooked, remove it from the pot and set aside to rest in a warm place. Scrape the bottom of the pot with a spatula to lift any caramelized cooking juices.

Place the cooked vegetables, milk and pan juices in a blender or mouli-légumes and blend to a smooth sauce about the thickness of double (heavy) cream. If the sauce is too liquid, reduce it by simmering briefly. Do not add any flour or cornflour (cornstarch), please, or your sauce will become floury, lumpy and gluey.

Slice the pork and place it in a serving dish with the pieces slightly overlapping. Cover with the hot creamy sauce and serve!

Serves 6–8

1.5 kg/3 lb pork loin, or other lean, boneless cut

6 tbsp butter

3 tbsp olive oil

3 medium carrots, roughly chopped

3 sticks celery, roughly chopped

3 medium onions, roughly chopped

milk, to cover

4–5 bay leaves

4–5 fresh sage leaves

1 tsp nutmeg, grated

salt and pepper

My Secrets

Remember that milk burns easily. Use a heavy-based pan to make the temperature easier to control. Don't be surprised if the milk curdles while cooking – after blending it will be smooth again.

Do not forget the nutmeg, an ingredient that is indispensable in most savoury milk dishes.

This dish can be made in advance and assembled just before serving. Reheat the meat (previously sliced and wrapped in foil) in the oven, and reheat the sauce separately in a saucepan.

Pollo Ripieno con Pistacchi e Pinoli

Chicken stuffed with pine kernels and pistachio nuts

Serves 8

1 chicken, boned, about
1.2 kg/2½ lb

salt and pepper

300 g/10 oz/1½ cups
minced (ground) pork

120 g/4 oz/½ cup
mortadella or cooked ham,
minced

60 g/2 oz/¼–½ cup pine
kernels

60 g/2 oz/¼–½ cup
pistachio nuts

1 egg

6 tbsp single (light) cream

1 sprig rosemary, chopped

1 sprig sage, chopped

1 clove garlic, crushed

4 tbsp olive oil

This is a successful and popular dish and an excellent one with which to impress guests – as long as your butcher bones the chicken for you, you don't need to tell them how easy it was to prepare! Cooking one, two or three chickens requires much the same effort, so this dish is ideal for large numbers. Serve it warm, with its juices, or cold with mayonnaise for a summer picnic. For those allergic to nuts, pitted black olives are a nice substitute.

Preheat the oven to 180°C/350°F/Gas 4. Lay out the boned chicken, skin down, on the counter. Sprinkle with salt and pepper.

In a bowl, combine the minced pork, mortadella or ham, pine kernels, pistachio nuts, egg, cream, rosemary, sage, garlic and some salt and pepper. Mix thoroughly, kneading with your hands to blend all the ingredients together.

Place the stuffing in the open chicken, mainly in the centre, and close it up like a parcel, overlapping the skin slightly.

With your hands, shape and pat the chicken into the shape of a rugby ball, making sure that the stuffing is fully enclosed and no air bubbles are present. Using kitchen thread, tie the chicken to prevent it opening while cooking.

Place the chicken in a roasting tin seam-side down. Brush it with a little oil and bake for 1½ hours. To serve, slice the chicken straight across and serve with the pan juices.

My Secrets

To serve cold, when the chicken is cooked, remove it from the roasting tin and place it in another dish, with a dish on top of the chicken, and a weight on top of the upper dish (a pack of flour or sugar will do). Leave it until the meat has cooled. This helps the chicken remain compact.

When cold, it is easy to slice. If you want to reheat the chicken, wrap the sliced chicken in foil as if it were still in one piece, and place in the oven for 20–30 minutes. Place the hot chicken in a serving dish and the slices will stay together nicely.

Petti di Pollo con Salsina ai Capperi

Chicken breasts with caper sauce

This is a happy marriage but both parts of this recipe – fried crumbed meat and sophisticated sauce – can stand on their own. Serve the chicken with a green salad or on another occasion, make the caper sauce and serve it with any cold meat.

To make the sauce, heat the oil in a pan and gently sauté the onion. Add the anchovies and stir well until they dissolve. Add the capers, parsley, flour and 240 ml/8 fl oz/1 cup of water. Keep stirring until the sauce thickens and bubbles gently. Remove from the heat and add the vinegar. Set aside in a warm place.

To prepare the chicken, cut each breast in half horizontally to give a total of 8 thin escalopes. Pound the chicken until flat and thin.

In a bowl, beat the egg lightly with a fork and season with salt and pepper. Marinate the chicken in the egg for 10 minutes, then coat each piece in breadcrumbs, pressing with your hand to make sure that the crumbs stick well to the meat.

Take a frying pan large enough to hold at least 4 escalopes with no overlapping. Pour enough oil into the pan to give a depth of about 2.5 cm/1 in. Wait until the oil is sizzling, then fry the first batch of escalopes on one side until golden. Turn them over and continue cooking until golden on the other side.

Drain the cooked chicken on kitchen paper to remove the excess oil. Meanwhile, fry the remaining chicken in the same way. Serve warm with the caper sauce.

Serves 4–6

For the sauce:

3 tbsp oil

½ medium onion, finely chopped

2 anchovies, packed in oil

2 tbsp salt-preserved capers, rinsed and chopped

2 tbsp parsley, chopped

1 tbsp plain (all-purpose) white flour, sifted

1 tsp balsamic vinegar

For the chicken:

4 chicken breast fillets, skinned

1 large egg

salt and pepper

300 g/10 oz/1½ cups dried breadcrumbs

vegetable oil, for frying

My Secrets

Slicing the chicken breasts into escalopes is not difficult, or dangerous. Use your hand to put pressure on the breast as you slice through it – you should be able to feel the blade going through the breast easily. Using a wet knife blade makes the job much easier too, as it prevents sticking.

The oil must be really hot when the escalopes go in to seal it well, otherwise the chicken will be greasy and soggy.

To avoid having a sauce that is too salty, rinse the capers under running water a few times.

Involtini di Pollo al Vino Bianco

Chicken mini rolls with Parmesan cheese, fresh sage and white wine

Serves 6

6 small chicken breasts, skinned and boned

12 slices of Italian raw ham

12 leaves sage

100 g/3 oz/¾ cup Parmesan cheese, in flakes

240 ml/8 fl oz/1 cup dry white wine

4 tbsp butter

4 tbsp of olive oil

plain (all-purpose) white flour, for coating

salt and pepper, to taste

This is a nice alternative to the usual escalopes. It can be prepared in advance and reheated with no risk that the meat becomes tough. It makes an impressive main course, served with mashed potatoes (see page 110), or spring peas and ham (see page 107).

Each chicken breast should be cut across into two very thin escalopes. (For this method, see the recipe for Petti di Pollo con Salsina ai Capperi (Chicken breasts with caper sauce) on page 81). Pound the meat gently to make it really thin. Season each slice with salt and pepper, lay on top a thin slice of ham, some flakes of Parmesan cheese, and a fresh sage leaf.

Roll up the meat and close it with a cocktail stick. Leave aside.

In a large saucepan melt the butter with the olive oil. When hot, coat lightly each roll with plain flour, and sauté the rolls on all sides in order to seal them.

When all the rolls are looking golden, splash them with a glass of dry white wine, let the alcohol evaporate and then cover and let it simmer until cooked. It will take about 10 to 15 minutes.

Add a little water in case the gravy becomes too thick, and the meat sticks to the pan.

Remember to pull the sticks out before serving!

My Secrets

When sealing the rolls in the pan, do it in one layer only. If your pan is not big enough for all the rolls, cook them in batches. When they are all sealed, return them to the pan, and now you can have more than one layer, when you add the wine and the water.

To make the Parmesan flakes, use a potato peeler. It makes the job very easy. Do not use any other cheese for this recipe, as it would completely change the final blend of flavours.

Petti di Pollo alla Valdostana

Chicken breasts with fontina and Italian ham

Fontina is a semi-mature cheese that is typical of Val d'Aosta, a small region at the foot of the White Mountain, on the border with the French Alps. The combination of ham and fontina is delicious: the cheese melts as the meat is cooked. A final touch of white truffle will make this dish into a real gourmet delicacy.

Use a broad, sharp knife and wet its blade to prevent sticking. Cut each breast horizontally but not completely through, so that it opens out to a butterfly shape. Carefully pound each breast until thin, but with the 'wings' still in one piece.

On one wing of each piece of chicken, lay a slice of fontina, then a slice of ham, leaving a small border of uncovered chicken. Season with pepper then fold the other wing of the butterfly over so that the two sides of the chicken touch each other, and press down to seal like a parcel.

Beat the egg in a shallow bowl and season with salt and pepper. Dust the parcels with flour, dip them in the beaten egg and then coat in the breadcrumbs, pressing to make sure that the crumbs stick well to the chicken and the parcel is well sealed.

In a frying pan large enough to hold the 4 breasts in one layer, melt the butter and enough oil to give a depth of 2.5 cm/1 in of fat in the pan. When the fat is sizzling hot, fry the breasts on each side until golden. Remove them to kitchen paper to drain.

Serve while still hot, as the cheese is melting. If you like truffles, and you are willing to be decadent, you can slice some white truffle on top before serving.

Serves 4

4 chicken breast fillets, skinned

4 thin slices fontina cheese

4 slices prosciutto

1 large egg, beaten

2 tbsp plain (all-purpose) white flour

210 g/7 oz/1¾ cups dried breadcrumbs

4 tbsp butter

about 150 ml/5 fl oz/⅔ cup vegetable oil

a few flakes of white truffle (optional)

salt and pepper

My Secrets

When you close the chicken parcel, make sure there is no cheese sticking out as it would melt in the pan while frying.

Use the palm of your hand, flat, to press the breadcrumbs onto the meat. The result will be much crispier.

If the cooking fat isn't really hot, the chicken will absorb it, with a greasy, soggy result. Make sure the fat is hot enough by testing its temperature. Drop a pinch of breadcrumbs in the frying pan and if they sizzle, it is ready.

Petti di Pollo alla Panna e Rosmarino

Chicken breasts with rosemary and cream

Serves 4

4 chicken breast fillets, skinned

plain (all-purpose) white flour, for coating

4 tbsp butter

2 tbsp olive oil

150 ml/5 fl oz/½–⅔ cup whipping (light whipping) cream

2 sprigs rosemary

salt and freshly ground black pepper

When I prepare for outside catering this recipe is one of the most successful. The combination of cream and rosemary is heavenly and makes an interesting alternative to classic escalopes, whether for a dinner party or a family meal.

Prepare the chicken breasts as in the recipe for Petti di Pollo con Salsina ai Capperi (Chicken breasts with caper sauce on page 71). When the chicken is flattened and ready to cook, coat it lightly with flour.

Heat the butter and oil in a frying pan. When sizzling, place the chicken in the pan in one layer with no overlapping. Brown well on one side before turning it over. If there is not enough room in the pan, cook the chicken in batches using the same pan.

When all the escalopes are brown, return them to the pan, still over a high heat, and add the cream and 150 ml/5 fl oz/½-⅔ cup of water. Bring to a boil, then add the rosemary and lower the heat to a simmer for a few minutes to allow the herb to infuse.

Remove and discard the rosemary sprigs, place the chicken in a serving dish and pour over the sauce. Serve with salt and freshly ground black pepper on top.

My Secret

The escalopes should be really thin and browned well on both sides before adding the cream. If the escalopes look white (chicken breast meat is white) the final dish will look very pale and unappetising.

This dish can be made in advance and reheated just before serving.

Rotolo di Tacchino Ripieno

Roasted roll of turkey breast

The original version of this recipe is made from veal. When I was living in Milan, I could ask my butcher to prepare a large slice of veal and pound it to 3 cm or ⅓ in thick. Turkey is more readily available in England, and it is a very good alternative to veal. This recipe is ideal for a sophisticated dinner but easier to make than it sounds.

In a bowl, beat the eggs with the Parmesan cheese and season with salt and pepper. In a medium non-stick frying pan, melt half the butter. When sizzling, pour in the egg mixture and cook over a medium heat until the egg is set. Set the omelette aside.

Lay the turkey breast out on a board and season with salt and pepper. Lay the slices of mortadella or ham on top. Squeeze the spinach to extract all the water and place it over the meat in an even layer. Lay the omelette on top.

Roll up, keeping the roulade tight and compact. Tie the roll gently with some kitchen string or thick cotton thread.

Melt the remaining butter and the oil in a heavy casserole. When hot, put the roulade in the pot and seal it all over. When golden, splash it with the wine and allow the wine to evaporate.

Lower the heat, add the rosemary and sage and simmer, covered, on the hob for about 40 minutes, adding water as necessary to keep the bottom of the pot moist.

Remove the meat from the pot, and leave it to cool before removing the string. Slice it with a very sharp knife and lay the slices in an ovenproof serving dish. Pour over the gravy from the pot and cover with foil.

Place in the oven to warm up before serving. Sauté potatoes are an ideal accompaniment to this dish.

Serves 4

2 large eggs

2 tbsp Parmesan cheese, grated

salt and pepper

4 tbsp butter

1 turkey breast, about 400 g/14 oz, cut as a large slice about 1 cm/⅓ in thick

4 thin slices mortadella or Parma ham

500 g/1 lb/2½ cups frozen spinach, defrosted

3 tbsp olive oil

120 ml/4 fl oz/½ cup dry white wine

2 sprigs rosemary

4 sage leaves

My Secrets

When laying the other ingredients on top of the turkey breast, leave a small border of turkey uncovered. This will make it easier to roll it up and will prevent the fillings slipping out when rolling.

The string is meant only to hold the roll together. Do not tie it too tightly or the string will cut into the turkey.

Arrosto di Tacchino

Roasted turkey breast

Serves 4–6

4 tbsp butter

4 tbsp olive oil

1 kg/2 lb turkey breast

120 ml/4 fl oz/½ cup dry white wine

2 sprigs rosemary

5 fresh sage leaves

salt and pepper

Here is a good basic example of the pot-roasting technique. While it is simple, not many people know how to do it properly – so that the meat is juicy, tender and very tasty. Giuditta taught me how to do this roast just right! It is a very good alternative to Britain's classic Sunday roast and can be served with all the usual vegetables and potatoes.

In a large casserole, heat the butter and oil until sizzling. Add the turkey and seal it on all sides – you must allow the meat to brown before you turn it over using a spatula rather than a fork, so that the meat is not pierced. When it is all browned, splash with the white wine and let the alcohol evaporate.

Once the meat and its juices are cooking gently over a medium-low heat, add the rosemary and sage and season with salt and pepper. Cover the pan, turn the heat down and leave to simmer gently for about 1 hour, checking occasionally that there is around 2.5 cm/1 in of liquid in the bottom of the casserole (if it starts to dry out, add half a glass of water, just to keep the pot moist).

A joint of 1 kg/2 lb will take about 1 hour to cook. When done, carve the turkey and serve it with the pan juices on a warmed serving dish.

My Secret

Turkey breast is a very lean cut with no waste. Ask your butcher to give you a large skinless turkey breast in one piece. It can weigh between 500 g/1 lb and 1.8 kg/4 lb.

Use a heavy-bottomed casserole so that the meat cooks evenly.

Saltimbocca alla Romana

Veal escalopes 'Roman style'

Saltimbocca means 'jump in your mouth'. Like most Italian dishes, it is a regional recipe and this one is from the Rome area. The combination of veal, prosciutto and sage is very nice.

Pound each escalope with a meat pounder or mallet and season with pepper. Lay a slice of prosciutto and a fresh sage leaf on top of each escalope and thread the 3 ingredients together with a cocktail stick.

In a large frying pan that can contain all the escalopes in one layer (tight, but one layer), heat the butter and oil and quickly fry the escalopes, sage side down first.

When you see that the fat of the ham is starting to melt, and the sage is frying, turn the escalopes over and fry on the other side for 1–2 minutes, maximum.

Pour the white wine into the pan and let it evaporate quickly over a very high heat. Season to taste and serve immediately on a warm serving dish.

Serves 4

8 small veal escalopes, 0.6 cm/¼ inch thick

salt and pepper

8 thin slices prosciutto

8 fresh sage leaves

4 tbsp butter

2 tbsp olive oil

120 ml/4 fl oz/½ cup white wine

My Secrets

The escalopes should be quite small, almost bite-sized.

After pouring the wine into the pan, depending on the quality of the meat, you might find that there is a little too much liquid. In this case, remove the meat from the pan and boil the juices over a very high heat until reduced. Return the meat to the pan and toss quickly to coat with the glossy juices.

This is a dish that does not like to wait, as veal tends to get tough if reheated or overcooked.

Scaloppine al Limone e Prezzemolo

Veal escalopes with lemon and parsley

Serves 6

2 tbsp butter

¾ tbsp olive oil

2 tbsp plain (all-purpose) white flour, for coating

6 veal escalopes, about 1 cm/⅓ in thick

juice of 1 large lemon

salt and pepper

2 tbsp parsley, chopped

The classic escalope is made of veal, but, if you prefer, a chicken breast is also perfect for this recipe. There are unlimited variations of this dish, but the procedure is always the same. Lemon and parsley is the classic 'scaloppina' and is probably the nicest of all. An escalope, by definition, must be thin and quite often the ones on sale are not thin enough, so pounding is the first step to a successful scaloppina.

In a large pan, heat the butter and oil until very hot. Lightly coat each escalope with flour and lay them in the pan over a very high heat. Wait until the first side is golden before you turn them over to brown on the other side.

Meanwhile, in a small bowl, dilute the lemon juice by adding the equivalent of one-third its volume in water. Add the diluted lemon juice to the pan and continue cooking over a very high heat until the sauce thickens, while scraping the bottom of the pan to incorporate the cooking juices. This should take about 7 minutes.

Season with salt and pepper, sprinkle with the chopped parsley and serve immediately while very hot.

My Secrets

The success of this dish depends on cooking the veal quickly.

Depending on the quality of veal you use, it may, while cooking, release a lot of juice and shrink. If this happens, remove the cooked escalopes from the pan and reduce the juices on their own. Then, return the escalopes to the pan to warm through, making sure they are coated in the sauce, and finish with the parsley and seasoning.

In every Italian kitchen you'll find an indispensable gadget, the meat pounder or mallet. With it you can thin the escalopes much better than with a rolling pin, which may tear the meat.

Spezzantino di Manzo Aromatico

Spicy casserole of beef with cream

This is classic 'comfort food'. It is perfect if prepared in advance, then reheated. I like to serve this dish at large parties, when people put their plates on their laps, and using a knife is not convenient. This casserole can be accompanied simply by boiled new potatoes.

In a large casserole, heat the oil and butter together. Brown (sear) the meat well, then add the chopped vegetables and cook on a medium heat for 10 minutes. Add the white wine and beef stock.

Season with salt and pepper, then add the spices, tomato paste and herbs. Simmer or pop in a moderate oven preheated to 180°C/350°F/ Gas 4, covered, for about 50 minutes. Check from time to time that there is plenty of liquid with the meat, if necessary adding a little extra stock.

Remove the meat from the casserole and keep warm. Leave the casserole on the heat and add the cream, scraping off all the bits clinging to the bottom and sides with a spoon. Return the meat to the casserole to coat it with sauce, then serve piping hot.

Serves 4

3 tbsp olive oil

60 g/2 oz/½ stick butter

1 kg/2¼ lb chuck steak, cut into 2 cm/1 in cubes

2 medium onions, finely chopped

2 medium carrots, finely chopped

1 large celery stalk, finely chopped

180 ml/6 fl oz/¾ cup dry white wine

225 ml/8 fl oz/1 cup beef stock

salt and pepper

1 clove, crushed

1 tsp coriander (cilantro) leaves, chopped

1/2 tsp ground cinnamon

1 tbsp concentrated tomato purèe (paste)

1 tsp chilli powder

100 ml/4 fl oz/½ cup whipping (light whipping) cream

My Secret

A heavy metal or terracotta casserole dish will guarantee the best results. If you have an Aga, you can cook this dish in the slow oven (or in a slow cooker) for double the time given above.

Some people find the taste of cinnamon a bit too powerful. it can be left out to make the dish less aromatic.

Spezzatino di Vitello al Pomodoro

Braised veal in tomato sauce

Serves 6

1/5 kg/3 lb boneless veal shoulder, cut into 2.5 cm/1 in cubes

3 tbsp plain (all-purpose) flour

3 tbsp olive oil

60 g/2 oz/½ stick butter

1 small onion, chopped

salt and pepper

120 ml/4 fl oz/¼ cup dry white wine

200 g/7 oz/1 cup frozen peas

500 ml/1 pint/2½ cups passata, or sieved tomatoes

2 large potatoes, peeled and cut into 2.5 cm/1 in cubes

Giuditta, my first husband's housekeeper and cook, used to do this spezzatino meaning, literally, veal stew. But 'stew' doesn't do justice to this dish, which is one of the nicest and simplest you can prepare. Giuditta surrounded the dish with a sort of magic when she was preparing it but, eventually, I managed to get the recipe!

Lightly coat the meat with flour. In a casserole, heat the oil and butter together over a medium heat and brown (sear) the meat on all sides, in batches.

Remove the meat from the casserole. Cook the onion gently in the oil and butter that remains in the casserole. Season with salt and pepper. When the onion starts to turn translucent, return the meat to the pot and add the wine, cooking for a few minutes. Scrape all the bits from the sides and bottom of the casserole.

Add the peas, still frozen, and the tomatoes. Simmer this mixture, covered, for about 1 hour, adding a little water or stock from time to time to keep everything moist.

Add the potatoes to the casserole about 30 minutes before the end of the cooking time. Serve piping hot.

My Secret

Some people cook the potatoes with the peas, with the unpleasant result that they mash. Adding them to the casserole just 30 minutes before the dish is ready keeps them slightly firm, which gives a much better result.

Costine di Vitello Piccanti

Veal chops with hot peppers

The smell wafting from your kitchen as you cook this recipe will take you straight to the heart of Italy – perhaps to the beach on a warm summer day. One of my favourite veal dishes, this also works well with chicken breast.

Heat 2 tablespoons olive oil in a large frying pan. Add the pepper and onion. Cook very gently for about 20 minutes until they soften without colouring. Add the olives, capers and tomatoes. Season with chilli and salt.

In the meantime, fry the garlic in the remaining oil. Add the anchovies, keeping the heat quite low to allow the anchovies to disintegrate, stirring. Add the cooked peppers to this paste, toss and keep warm.

Heat the butter in a pan large enough to take all the veal chops in a single layer. In the meantime, lightly coat the meat with flour. Fry the chops on both sides over a high heat to brown (sear).

Turn the heat down to allow the veal to cook without burning. If necessary, add a little water to keep the veal moist. Season with salt.

Add the pepper sauce, covering the meat completely. Toss well, bring to a sizzle and serve.

Serves 6

3 tbsp olive oil

2 red bell peppers, cored and cut into thin strips

2 yellow bell peppers, cored and cut into thin strips

1 small onion, chopped

1 tbsp green olives, chopped

1 tbsp capers in salt, rinsed

3 tomatoes, blanched, skinned, deseeded and diced

1 tsp dried chilli

salt

1 clove garlic, chopped

2 anchovies

60 g/2 oz/½ stick butter

6 veal chops, each about 150 g/5 oz

2 tbsp plain (all-purpose) white flour

My Secrets

Veal may become tough when overcooked. Depending on the thickness of each chop, they should take no longer than 8 minutes to cook on each side.

This dish is so tasty that a simple side salad is the only accompaniment you will need.

Medaglioni di Agnello al Cognac

Lamb medallions with Cognac sauce

Serves 4

3 tbsp olive oil

8 lamb medallions

90 ml/3 fl oz/¼-½ cup
Cognac or brandy

180 ml/6 fl oz/¾ cup strong
red wine

½ stock cube

90 ml/3 fl oz/½ cup single
(light) cream

1 tsp coarse ground
pepper

salt

*I cook this dish for dinner parties and it is always a great success.
The only difficulty is guessing when the lamb is pink and ready to
serve. It is difficult to give precise timing because of the thickness of
the medallions. I suggest that you practice for your family before
serving to an important guest!*

Heat the oil in a large saucepan and saute the lamb medallions on
both sides until golden. This will take 10–15 minutes, depending on
their thickness. Splash the medallions with the Cognac and cook until
it has evaporated, then remove the lamb from the pan and keep
warm on a serving dish.

Add the red wine and the stock cube to the juices in the pan, then
simmer until the liquid has reduced by half.

Add the cream and pepper, then stir well. Season with salt as
necessary and return the meat to the pan, turning it to ensure that it
is well coated with the sauce.

Place the lamb on a serving dish, pour the sauce over and
serve immediately.

My Secret
Do not overcrowd the pan. Make sure the heat remains very high
while browning (searing) the meat, so that it browns well before you
continue cooking.

Filetto di Maiale Ripieno

Stuffed fillet of pork with sun-dried tomatoes and sultanas

This is a great recipe for the Christmas season, as it is impressive yet easy – and a little bit different from the usual turkey.

Cut into the pork fillet lengthways (but not all the way through), then open like a book. Pound it gently, then season with salt and pepper.

Place the sun-dried tomatoes on the meat, add the sultanas and sage leaves. Close the 'book' and tie with string into its original shape.

Heat the oil and butter together gently, add the meat and brown (sear) on all sides. Splash with the Marsala, reserved from soaking the sultanas, and allow to evaporate.

Place the pork in a casserole and cook, covered, in an oven preheated to 170°C/325°F/Gas 3 for 30–40 minutes, basting from time to time.

To make the sauce, remove the meat from the pan and add the wine to the juices. Cook until hot and bubbling. Reduce the heat and add the cream, stirring until thick and blended. Adjust the seasoning to taste.

Slice the pork and serve at once with the sauce spooned over.

Serves 4

750 g/1½ lb pork fillet

salt and pepper

6 sun-dried tomatoes, halved lengthways

2 tbsp sultanas, soaked in Marsala for 2 hours, or overnight

6 fresh sage leaves

60 g/2 oz/½ stick butter

90 ml/3 fl oz/¼ cup white wine

2 tbsp whipping (light whipping) cream

My Secret

This dish is most fragrant if served as soon as it is cooked. Reheating makes the meat a bit dry.

When slicing, do it diagonally in order to get bigger slices. It will look more impressive!

Anatra all' Arancia con Salvia e Pancetta

Pot-roasted duck with orange, sage and pancetta

Serves 4

1 duck, weighing about
2–2.5 kg/4–5 lb

4–5 slices smoked
pancetta

2 large juicy oranges,
halved

4–5 fresh sage leaves

2 tbsp olive oil

60 g/2 oz/½ stick butter

125 ml/4 fl oz/¼–½ cup
brandy

salt and pepper

orange rind, to garnish

Duck is a good alternative to chicken and, for a dinner party, is a little more sophisticated. As this is quite a rich dish, I would serve it with something very plain, such as boiled or roasted new potatoes.

Wash the duck inside and out under tap water, then pat dry with kitchen paper (paper towels). Place the pancetta, orange and 2 sage leaves inside the duck's cavity.

Heat the oil and butter together in an ovenproof roasting tin just big enough to hold the duck over a medium heat. Brown (sear) the duck on all sides. When the duck is brown all over and the oil starts to smoke, add the juice of ½ an orange and the remaining sage. Cover with a tight-fitting lid and transfer to a moderate oven preheated to 180°C/350°F/Gas 4.

After 30 minutes, add the juice of the remaining orange, then return to the oven, removing the lid. Cook the duck for a further 1 hour, basting occasionally with juices from the pan. Remove the duck from the pan and reserve.

Using a spoon, remove and discard most of the fat remaining in the pan. Add the brandy to the pan, scraping with a spatula to mix in any bits that may be clinging to the base and the sides. Simmer the mixture for a few minutes to blend everything together. Season with salt and pepper.

Return the duck to the pan and coat it well with the brandy sauce. Remove the duck and carve it at the table, garnishing with orange rind to serve.

My Secrets

For a really orangey taste, grate some of the orange rind and add it to the orange juice while cooking.

When doubling the quantities for this recipe, do not double the amount of orange juice as it would be too liquid. I suggest using 3 oranges instead of 4 and 175 ml/6 fl oz brandy.

Fegato alla Veneziana
Venetian-style calves liver

Calves' liver is one of those foods that you either love or hate. In Italy it is very popular and considered to be very healthy, as it is rich in iron and minerals. If you have never cooked calves' liver, remember that it becomes tough and rubbery if it is over-cooked. This recipe is a classic, ideal served with mashed potatoes or polenta to soak up all of the delicious juices.

Using a very sharp knife, slice the liver very thinly into long strips.

In a large frying pan, heat 4 tablespoons of oil and add the sliced onions. Cook for about 25 minutes over a medium heat, stirring frequently, until the onions become wilted and lightly golden. Remove the onions and reserve.

In the same pan, add the remaining oil and, when sizzling hot, add the strips of liver. Cook it by tossing it with two spatulas (one in each hand) for about 5 minutes until it loses its pink colour. When the liver starts looking brown, with a little bit of crispiness on the outside, add all the onions and cook them together for a few minutes.

Transfer to a serving platter. Add the butter to the empty pan and melt it over a medium heat, scraping all the bits from the bottom and sides the pan.

When the butter is melted, pour this sauce on to the liver and onions. Season with salt and pepper, garnish with chopped parsley and serve hot.

Serves 6

1 kg /2¼ lb calves' liver

6 tbsp olive oil

3 large onions, very thinly sliced

60 g/2 oz/¼ cup butter

salt and pepper

3 tbsp parsley, finely chopped

My Secret
When cooking onions, adding a little salt will make them release their juices, and wilt more easily without burning.

Some people like to splash a few drops of Balsamic vinegar on the cooked liver before serving.

Vegetables and Salads

The art of making salads

Italians eat lots of salads, whether as part of a main dish, served as a starter, or as a side dish. You might be surprised to hear that in Italy there are not as many 'declared vegetarians' as in the United Kingdom or the United States. Italian cooking has a vast range of dishes made only from vegetables that there is almost no need to become vegetarian.

When preparing vegetable dishes and salads, the quality and freshness of the ingredients that you choose is paramount. Choose those that are in season: you will spend less and eat better! Do not even try to make stuffed tomatoes in winter, as you will be disappointed. For the same reason, do not bother with Savoy cabbage in summer, as it will taste bitter and rubbery. If you have been in restaurants in Italy, you might remember that oil and vinegar bottles are left on the table. This simple habit reveals a lot about Italian salad dressings: a good olive oil mixed with strong wine vinegar (red or white, or balsamic if preferred) is all you need to dress the best salad. All seasonings are added at the very last minute, just before serving, to prevent the salad from wilting. Vinaigrette should never be prepared in advance. The acidity of the vinegar will interfere with the chemistry of the oil.

It is difficult to give precise quantities for a salad dressing as it depends on the strength of the oil and the vinegar. In the following recipes you will find some good secrets to take you through the art of salad making.

Funghi Trifolati
Sautéed mushrooms

The best and most tasty mushrooms you can find in Italy are porcini, also called ceps. Autumn is the best season to eat them, they will be fresh and on the menu of almost every Italian restaurant. When fresh mushrooms are not available, the dried ones are fine to use. They are very expensive, even in Italy, so for this recipe I use chestnut mushrooms, or brown mushrooms, with a good portion of dried mushrooms added to give that great flavour without spending a fortune. This is a basic recipe that always works.

Place the dried mushrooms in a small bowl. Cover them with hot water and leave to soak for at least 30 minutes. Meanwhile, clean and slice the fresh mushrooms and set them aside.

In a frying pan, sauté the garlic in the olive oil. Add the fresh mushrooms and sauté for a few minutes until they begin to wilt. Use your fingers to lift the dried mushrooms from their soaking water and add them to the pan. Stir gently and allow the mushrooms to sweat for a few minutes.

Strain the soaking water through a muslin cloth or kitchen paper and add it to the frying pan. Cover the pan and simmer the mushrooms very gently until the water evaporates.

Add the parsley, season to taste with salt and pepper and serve.

Serves 6

60 g/2 oz/4 level tbsp
dried porcini mushrooms

500 g/1 lb/2½ cups
chestnut mushrooms

2 cloves garlic, sliced

6 tbsp olive oil

1 tbsp parsley, chopped

salt and pepper

My Secrets
The quality of the mushrooms is essential. Some dried mushrooms are literally crumbs; some are nice big pieces, very white and meaty.

Soaking the mushrooms not only helps to rehydrate them, but also dislodges sand. This is why the water needs careful straining.

vegetables and salads

Finocchi Gratinati al Parmigiano

Grilled fennel with Parmesan cheese

Serves 6

4 large fennel bulbs, trimmed

6 tbsp butter

½ beef or chicken Italian stock cube

150 ml/5 fl oz/½–⅔ cup whole milk

½ tsp nutmeg, grated

salt and pepper

4 tbsp Parmesan cheese, grated

Fennel is best in winter and delicious eaten raw, thinly sliced in a salad or cooked. It is one of the most popular winter vegetables in Italy. This is a very simple way to cook fennel, yet very good and rather different from the usual steamed vegetables commonly found on British tables.

Trim off and discard the tops of the fennel. Cut each fennel bulb in quarters lengthways and wash under running water, checking that there is no grit between the layers. Drain and set aside.

In a pan large enough to hold all the fennel, melt the butter and when hot, add the fennel bulbs and brown them well on all sides.

When the butter is just about to burn, crumble the piece of stock cube into the pan and add the milk. Simmer gently, covered, for about 15–20 minutes, or until the milk reduces and the fennel starts to feel tender.

Stir the nutmeg into the fennel and season with salt and pepper. Transfer the mixture to an ovenproof serving dish. Sprinkle with the Parmesan cheese and grill for 2–3 minutes, until the cheese is melted. Serve immediately.

My Secret
The final dish should look golden and very appetising, so brown the fennel thoroughly in the butter before adding any milk to the pan. Adding the milk too early will poach the fennel instead.

Cavolo al Balsamico

Savoy cabbage with balsamic vinegar

Cabbage is at its best after the first frost. This recipe is from a friend with whom I spent a wonderful skiing holiday in Madesimo, on the Alps by the Swiss border. In that region cabbage is part of many recipes. This one is very simple and yet delicious. It is ideal served with braised sausages or with a pork roast because the sweetness of the pork is complimented by the distinctive taste of the cabbage.

Discard the outer leaves of the cabbage. Cut it into quarters and then into strips about 1 cm/½ in wide. Wash thoroughly and drain.

Bring a pot of water to the boil and, when the water is boiling, add 2 teaspoons of salt. Blanch the cabbage for a few minutes until it is wilted but still al dente. Drain and rinse immediately under cold running water.

In a large frying pan, melt the butter and fry the pancetta and garlic until the pancetta turns golden.

Turn the heat to maximum and add the drained blanched cabbage, tossing to coat the cabbage with the flavoured butter. Cook for 5 minutes until the cabbage turns golden. Season to taste with salt and freshly ground pepper.

Turn off the heat and add the balsamic vinegar, while tossing. Serve immediately.

Serves 6

1 medium Savoy cabbage

salt and pepper

6 tbsp butter

100 g/3½ oz/½ cup smoked pancetta, diced

3 cloves garlic, sliced

1 tbsp balsamic vinegar

My Secret
Never allow balsamic vinegar to cook because it loses its flavour when heated.

If pancetta is not available, smoked streaky bacon will do.

Caponatina Siciliana

Sweet and sour aubergines (eggplant)

Serves 6–8

1 tbsp sultanas

1 tbsp salt-preserved capers

6 sticks green celery

500 g/1 lb/2½ cups aubergines (eggplant)

210 ml/7 fl oz/¾ cup olive oil

1 medium onion, chopped

210 ml/7 fl oz/¾ cup passata or sieved tomatoes

2 tbsp red wine vinegar

1 tbsp pine kernels

1 tsp sugar

120 g/4 oz/½ cup green pitted olives, chopped

5–6 basil leaves, chopped

salt

Caponatina is a very appetising dish that, like many Sicilian preparations, has some Arabian influence. There are several variations: in Siracusa they make it without tomato; in Palermo they add dark cocoa powder and orange zest to it. My version is a family recipe that was passed to me by a friend who lives in Messina. Vegetables are fried in olive oil and dressed with a thick tomato sauce seasoned with vinegar and a touch of sugar. It is a dish that is difficult to define; it can be a cooked salad, a side dish, an antipasto and a vegetarian main course, perhaps served with hard-boiled eggs. Caponatina is best if made in advance and served cold.

Place the sultanas in a small bowl, cover with water and leave to soak. Thoroughly wash the capers to remove the salt and set aside. Cut the aubergines (eggplant) into 2.5 cm/1 in cubes and the celery into pieces the size of a potato chip.

In a large frying pan, heat the oil and fry the celery until golden but still crunchy. Remove from the pan and set aside. In the same oil fry the aubergines (eggplant), tossing gently until soft.

In the remaining oil, cook the onion until golden. Add the passata and simmer for 2–3 minutes. Add the vinegar, pine kernels, sugar, the rinsed capers and the drained sultanas. Turn the heat off and leave for a few minutes, then mix.

In a large bowl mix the aubergines (eggplant), celery and pitted olives. Pour the tomato sauce on top and toss gently. Add the basil and season with a little salt. Serve cold.

My Secret
This dish is better prepared one day in advance, which gives all the flavours a chance to blend.

Pomodori Ripieni di Riso

Tomatoes stuffed with rice and fresh herbs

My ex-sister-in-law Marina is one of my best friends and an excellent cook. Going to her house for a summer supper was a real treat, and we would almost certainly find these delicious tomatoes on the table, picked from her vegetable garden. What is special about this recipe is that the rice is stuffed into the tomatoes before being cooked, and baked with the tomatoes in the oven. The result is a mix of different textures: the soft rice inside and the crunchy texture on the top. Serve as a starter or on a summer buffet table.

Preheat the oven to 180°C/350°F/Gas 4. Cut off the top of each tomato with a sharp knife and set it aside. This 'lid' will be used to enclose the tomatoes when they are stuffed.

Carefully scoop the pulp out of the tomatoes with a teaspoon and reserve it in a bowl.

Sprinkle the empty tomatoes with salt and lay them upside-down on a plate, so that they release some water.

Mix the crushed garlic with the tomato pulp, fresh herbs and 2 tablespoons of the olive oil. Season with salt and pepper. Place half the tomato pulp in the bottom of an ovenproof dish. Mix the raw rice with the remaining tomato pulp.

With some kitchen paper, carefully dry the inside of the tomatoes and stuff them with the rice mixture. Sprinkle with the remaining olive oil and top with the tomato 'lids'.

Place the tomatoes close together in the ovenproof dish and bake for 45 minutes. Serve at room temperature.

Serves 4

4 large tomatoes, firm and ripe

salt and pepper

1 clove garlic, crushed

2 tsp basil, chopped

2 tsp parsley, chopped

1 tsp mint, chopped

4 tbsp extra virgin olive oil

4 tbsp arborio rice

My Secrets

Do not decide to cook this recipe before going to the market. It only works with big round, ripe tomatoes that are still firm. If the tomatoes are too ripe and watery, they will turn mushy in the oven.

The tomatoes must fit snugly in the ovenproof dish. If they have too much room, they will collapse. The tomato pulp in the base of the dish keeps the stuffed tomatoes moist while cooking.

Arborio rice is best for this recipe. Other rices are less absorbent and will leave your dish very wet and watery.

Peperoni alla Griglia

Grilled bell peppers

3 red bell peppers

3 yellow bell peppers

4 cloves garlic, peeled and halved

8 basil leaves, plus extra to garnish

salt and pepper

extra virgin olive oil

Grilled bell peppers probably need no introduction as they have become very popular outside Italy in recent years. I have come across at least 8 different recipes, but this is the one I have grown up with and it has never let me down. Grilled bell peppers are ideal with grilled meat, but they also make an excellent starter, served with Parma ham or mozzarella. Choose heavy, unblemished, meaty peppers for this recipe.

Using a cast-iron grill-pan or an overhead grill (broiler), grill or broil the bell peppers, turning as necessary, until the skin is charred all over. When they are thoroughly blackened, remove them from the heat and set aside to cool on a tray.

Working over a bowl to catch the clear juices inside the peppers, pull out the stalk and tear the peppers in two. Remove and discard the black skin and the seeds.

Cut the flesh of the peppers into strips lengthways and place them in the bowl with the juices, garlic, basil and salt. Cover with the olive oil and marinate for several hours, tossing occasionally.

Just before serving, discard the garlic and garnish the dish with some more basil leaves.

My Secrets

The skins of the grilled peppers must be totally black, but the flesh should still be almost raw. Be very careful not to overcook the peppers as the flesh will lose its texture.

When turning the peppers over, use tongs to avoid piercing them and losing the tasty juices.

Do not wash the peppers after peeling them.

It is best to prepare the peppers one day in advance to allow their flavour to blend with those of the other ingredients.

Involtini di Melanzane

Aubergine (eggplant) rolls with Parma ham

These delicious rolls taste fresh and light and are very easy to prepare. They are ideal served as a starter, or part of a summer buffet. The best way to grill the aubergine (eggplant) slices is to use a cast-iron pan. Alternatively, you could barbecue them.

Heat the oven to 180°C/350°F/Gas 4.

Slice the aubergines (eggplant) lengthways about 1 cm/½ in thick – you should have 12 slices in total. Heat the cast-iron pan on top of the stove until it is very hot. Cook the aubergine (eggplant) slices dry for a few minutes on each side until they are wilted and bend easily. Use a pallet spatula to turn them over. Set aside on a plate.

In a mixing bowl, combine the Parmesan, breadcrumbs, olives, olive oil, lemon zest, basil, oregano and some salt and pepper. Spread this mixture on one side of the aubergine (eggplant) slices.

Roll up the aubergines (eggplant) with the filling to the inside, then wrap the rolls in a slice of Parma ham and fix with a cocktail stick. Place in an ovenproof dish and transfer to the oven for about 5 minutes. Serve warm or cold, as you prefer.

Serves 4–6

2 long aubergines (eggplant)

4 tbsp Parmesan cheese, grated

3 tbsp breadcrumbs

6–8 black olives, chopped

4 tbsp extra virgin olive oil

grated zest of 1 lemon

3–4 basil leaves, chopped

1 tsp dried oregano

salt and pepper

6–8 slices Parma ham

My Secret
To ensure aubergines (eggplant) are fresh, pick them up and apply a little pressure with your fingertips. If the flesh is firm and your finger doesn't leave a mark, the aubergine (eggplant) is a good one. If your finger leaves an indentation in the aubergine (eggplant), don't buy it. It is likely to be old, bitter and will give a disappointing result.

Parmigiana di Melanzane

Aubergines (eggplant) baked with tomato and cheese

Serves 4–6

4 large aubergines (eggplant)

salt and pepper

750 ml/1½ pints/3¼ cups vegetable oil

2 tbsp olive oil

½ small onion, chopped

240 ml/8 fl oz/1 cup passata or sieved tomatoes

2 balls Italian mozzarella, about 100 g/3½ oz/½ cup each, thinly sliced

1 large bunch fresh basil

8 tbsp Parmesan cheese, grated

There are several versions of this fabulous vegetarian dish. This recipe, which is my favourite, comes from Paola, my ex-mother-in-law's cook, who lived in Rome.

Cut the aubergines (eggplant) lengthways into 1 cm/⅓ in slices. Place in a large colander, sprinkle with salt and set aside for 30 minutes to remove any bitter juices. Rinse them under running water and pat the aubergines (eggplant) dry.

Heat the vegetable oil in a large frying pan and, working in batches, fry the slices of aubergine (eggplant) until golden on each side. Remove and set aside to drain on kitchen paper.

Place the olive oil and onion in a saucepan and fry gently over a medium heat until the onion starts to brown. Add the passata or sieved tomatoes, bring to a boil and simmer for 15 minutes. Season with salt and pepper and remove the pan from the heat.

Heat the oven to 180°C/350°F/Gas 4. Spread a large spoonful of the tomato sauce over the bottom of an ovenproof baking dish about 25 cm/10 in long. Lay enough aubergine (eggplant) slices in the dish to cover the bottom. Spread some tomato sauce on the aubergines (eggplant) and top with a few slices of mozzarella. Add a few leaves of basil and sprinkle with some of the Parmesan cheese.

Continue layering the aubergines (eggplant), tomato sauce, mozzarella, basil and Parmesan cheese until the dish is full – you should have at least three layers of aubergine (eggplant) and the top layer should be tomato sauce covered with mozzarella and basil.

Bake for about 1 hour. When cooked, remove from the oven and leave to rest for 20 minutes before serving.

My Secrets

Salting the aubergines (eggplant) to remove the bitter juices is necessary only if they are grown in the sun. If they are from a greenhouse, this step can be skipped.

Do not allow the aubergines (eggplant) to overlap in the frying pan, and cook them in batches to ensure each slice is cooked evenly.

Use tongs to turn the aubergines (eggplant) when frying as piercing them with a fork while frying will make them very greasy. You can use grilled aubergines instead of fried ones, but they are not as delicious.

Pisellini al Prosciutto

Spring peas with ham

This method of cooking peas is very versatile. From this basic recipe, which is ideal served as a side vegetable, you can turn it into a pasta sauce (by adding some cream), or to a soup (by adding a good chicken stock). What is essential is the first step with pancetta and onion. Using frozen peas is not a compromise as long as you use petits pois, the very small spring peas. I always use frozen peas, even in spring, even in Italy! Invariably I find them very nice and tender, so do not believe it is worth taking the time to prepare the fresh ones.

In a small saucepan, heat the butter or oil and add the pancetta and onion. Sauté until the pancetta is translucent and the onion starts to turn golden.

Add the frozen peas and a little cold water: enough to cover the base of the pan by about 1 cm/½ in. Simmer, covered, until the peas are tender, and the water has completely evaporated – this will take about 15–20 minutes from the time when the peas have thawed. Season to taste and serve.

Serves 6

3 tbsp butter or
olive oil

90 g/3 oz/⅓ cup pancetta,
diced

½ medium onion, chopped

500 g/1 lb/2½ cups frozen
petits pois or spring peas

salt and pepper

My Secrets
The skin of peas gets tough if salt is added while cooking.
Always salt just before going to the table.

The peas should be cooked from frozen to keep them tender.

Sometimes fresh peas sit on the supermarket shelf for a few days and become tough, whereas the frozen peas are always sweet and tender.

Torta di Verdure
Vegetable pie

Serves 8

For the pastry:

210 g/7 oz/1 cup plain (all-purpose) white flour

210 g/7 oz/1 cup semolina flour

210 g/7 oz/1 cup butter, at room temperature

2 whole eggs, plus 1 yolk extra for glazing

For the filling:

4 tbsp butter

1 kg/2 lb/5 cups frozen spinach

4 small cloves garlic, sliced

2–3 courgettes (zucchini)

2 tbsp olive oil

1 tsp thyme, fresh or dried

salt and pepper

4 eggs

1 smoked mozzarella or scamorza, about 100 g/3½ oz/½ cup, finely sliced

The beauty of this pie is the combination of plain (all-purpose) flour and semolina in the pastry, making it extra crunchy. This recipe includes spinach and courgettes (zucchini), but you can create your own pie with almost any vegetable: peas and carrots, aubergines (eggplant) and mint, baby artichokes or mushrooms. It is a versatile dish that can be served as a starter or main course or buffet lunch.

To make the pastry, put all ingredients in a food processor. Add 3 tablespoons of cold water (less if the eggs are large) and mix well to form a dough. Wrap in cling film and place in the fridge to rest while you prepare the vegetables.

To make the filling, melt the butter in a frying pan and sweat the spinach and half the garlic until all the water exuded by the spinach has evaporated.

Slice the courgettes (zucchini) into discs about 0.5 cm/¼ in thick. In a separate pan, sauté them with the oil and remaining garlic until tender. Mix the two vegetables, add the thyme and season with salt and pepper. Set aside.

Preheat the oven to 180°C/350°F/Gas 4. Roll out two-thirds of the pastry into a circle large enough to cover the base and sides of a 20 cm/8 in springform tin. Pour the vegetables into the pastry and make four indentations in the mixture. Break the eggs into these holes, then cover the vegetables and eggs with mozzarella.

Roll out the rest of the pastry to make a lid for the pie and seal it carefully with your fingers. Pierce the pastry top with a fork to let the steam escape and glaze with the egg yolk. Bake for 1 hour and 15 minutes. Leave the pie to rest for 10–15 minutes before serving.

My Secrets

If you can't find a smoked mozzarella, a plain one will do.

When covering the pie with the pastry lid, make sure you carefully seal the sides of the pastry to the top to prevent any leakage.

Before opening the springform tin, check that the top of the pastry doesn't hang over the sides of the tin. If it does, gently pare away the excess before opening the tin to prevent the pie top cracking.

Ensure that the vegetables do not retain lots of moisture during the initial cooking phase as this will make the bottom of the pie soggy.

Torta di Patate alle Mandorle

Potato cake with almonds

Torta di Patate is a savoury cake that makes an excellent main course when served with a side salad. It can be served at room temperature or warm, with a tomato sauce.

In a pot, boil the potatoes in their skins for about 40 minutes or until tender. Peel them while still hot and mash using a ricer. Mix the beaten eggs and chopped herbs into the mash, season to taste with salt and pepper and set aside.

Heat 1 tablespoon of the olive oil in a frying pan and sauté the courgettes (zucchini). Season with salt and pepper. Cook the carrots and onions separately in the same way, using another tablespoon of olive oil for each vegetable.

Coat a 20 cm/8 in springform mould with butter and breadcrumbs to prevent the potato cake sticking to the mould.

Heat the oven to 180°C/350°F/Gas4. Use two-thirds of the potato mixture to line the base and sides of the mould. Layer the vegetables in the mould, sprinkling plenty of Parmesan cheese and seasoning with pepper between each layer.

Cover the last layer of vegetables with the remaining potato mixture. Sprinkle the flaked almonds evenly over the top of the pie and bake for 1 hour. Remove from the oven and leave the pie to rest for 20 minutes before serving.

Serves 6

1.5 kg/3½ lb/5¼ cups potatoes

2 eggs, beaten

1 tbsp fresh basil, chopped

1 tbsp fresh marjoram, chopped

1 tbsp fresh thyme, chopped

salt and pepper

3 tbsp extra virgin olive oil

300 g/10 oz/1½ cups courgettes (zucchini), sliced

300 g/10 oz/1½ cups carrots, sliced

500 g/1 lb/2 cups onions, sliced

butter, for greasing the tin

breadcrumbs, for coating the tin

9 tbsp Parmesan cheese, grated

60 g/2 oz/4 level tbsp flaked almonds

My Secret

When handling mashed potatoes, wet your hands with cold water so that the potatoes do not stick to your hands.

It is important to leave the pie to rest after baking; if it is too hot, it will not hold its shape when sliced.

Pure' di Patate

Mashed potatoes

Serves 6

1 kg/2 lb/5 cups potatoes, preferably Desirée, King Edward, Maris Piper or Yukon Gold

6 tbsp butter

300 ml/10 fl oz/1¼ cups milk

5 tbsp Parmesan cheese, grated

a pinch of nutmeg

salt and pepper

Mashed potatoes can seem quite basic and perhaps a little boring, but this recipe is so good that you can serve it as a side dish even at a very important dinner.

In a large saucepan or pot, boil the potatoes in their skins for 40–50 minutes or until tender. Drain the potatoes and, as soon as they are cool enough to handle, peel them.

Mash the potatoes with a ricer and return them to the same pan. Place over a low heat and add the butter. Meanwhile, in a small saucepan, bring the milk to a boil.

Using an electric whisk, beat the potatoes over the heat as you gradually add the hot milk and Parmesan cheese. Keep adding the milk and whisking until the potatoes have a creamy, mousse-like texture and begin to bubble.

Season the mash to taste with nutmeg, salt and pepper and serve immediately.

My Secrets

Using a ricer instead of a potato masher makes a big difference. The mash will be fluffy and light with no lumps.

Adding hot milk to the potatoes is also an important technique. There will be no lumps and the potatoes, beaten and cooked, will taste almost like a savoury mousse.

You can judge that the thickness of the mash is right by sticking a spoon into the centre of the pot – it should stay upright.

Frittata di Cipolle

Italian omelette with onions

Omelette is the French word for the Italian 'frittata'. But the difference is not only linguistic, in fact they are quite different. An omelette does not need to be turned over, instead it is usually folded in half so that it is soft inside and golden outside. Frittata is about an 2.5 cm/1 in thick and should be cooked through. In this recipe, which is served as a starter, I use onions, but it can be made with courgettes (zucchini) and other vegetables.

Heat the olive oil in a frying pan. Sauté the onions until they are translucent and beginning to turn golden. Sprinkle them with a little salt while cooking.

Break the eggs into a bowl, season with salt and pepper, then add the Parmesan cheese and milk and beat with a fork. Add the cooked onions, stir well and set aside.

In a non-stick pan about 20 cm/8 in in diameter, heat the butter, and swirl it evenly around the pan. When very hot, pour in the egg mixture and cook over a medium heat for 5–8 minutes, until you can see the mixture starting to thicken around the edges. Cover and cook for a few more minutes on a medium/low heat.

To turn the frittata over, take a plate that will fit into the pan and wet it to stop the egg sticking to it. Lay the plate, face down, onto the frittata. Then, holding the plate against the frittata, turn the pan upside down. The frittata will fall onto the plate and you can then slide it easily back into the pan cooked side up.

Continue cooking the frittata on the other side until it is completely done, about another 8 minutes. Remove from the heat and serve warm or cold with a side salad.

Serves 4

2 tbsp olive oil

4 large onions, sliced

2 large eggs

salt and pepper

2 tbsp Parmesan cheese, grated

2 tbsp milk

2 tbsp butter

My Secrets

You will notice that when the frying pan is crowded with onions, it is easy to cook them without burning. Sprinkling some salt on the onions causes them to release a little moisture, and that will make them cook even better.

A non-stick pan is indispensable to prevent the egg mixture sticking while cooking. Before you turn the Frittata over, separate the edges of the frittata from the pan, and then use the handle to shake the pan horizontally. This will detach the frittata from the bottom of the pan and it will be easy to turn it over.

Insalata di Pomodori Estivi

Summer tomato salad

Serves 6

6 large tomatoes –
approximately 1 kg /2 lb

3 tbsp extra virgin
olive oil

10 basil leaves

3 large cloves of garlic,
peeled

salt and pepper

This is one of the best ways to enjoy fresh, fragrant tomatoes which have ripened in the sun. It doesn't really matter what variety of tomatoes you select, as long as they are fully ripe and unblemished. My mother used to prepare this salad for us when we came back home from the beach and serve with some freshly baked bread.

Peel the tomatoes before slicing and deseeding. To do this easily, bring a pot of water to a boil and immerse the whole tomatoes, one at a time for a few seconds, in the boiling water. Transfer each tomato to a bowl of cold water to cool them quickly. After this process, the skin of the tomato will come off easily.

Cut the tomatoes in 2.5 cm/1 in chunks. You may find that the tomatoes are very seedy. In this case, discard the seeds, as they are indigestible and unpleasant tasting.

Dress the tomatoes with olive oil, the basil roughly torn by hand, and the garlic cloves cut in halves.

Let the tomatoes marinate for a few hours and season with salt and pepper just before serving.

Remove the garlic before taking to the table.

My Secrets

Don't marinate the salad in the fridge because the cold won't permit the flavours to come out and blend easily.

Always add salt just before serving. Early salting will cause the tomatoes to release their water.

Insalata di Riso 'Arlecchino'

Harlequin rice salad

In summer in almost every northern Italian home you may be served an 'Insalata di Riso' as an antipasto or a light lunch accompanied by some Parma ham. It is a great help to have this salad in the fridge on a hot day when you want something special to eat but do not feel like cooking. You will not find this in any other cookery book, as every household has its own version: this is my mother's recipe, which I now share with you.

In a large saucepan, bring some water to the boil, add the rice and cook for 15 minutes. Drain, then rinse under cold water and drain again thoroughly. Meanwhile, in a separate saucepan, hard boil the eggs, then cool and peel.

Place the drained rice in a large bowl. Dice the eggs and cooked ham and add them to the rice with the cheese, frankfurter, olives, bell peppers, sweetcorn, capers and pickled onions.

Dress with the lemon juice and olive oil. Chop the basil and stir it into the salad. Season the mixture to taste with salt and pepper and serve cold.

Serves 8

300 g/10 oz/1⅓ cups arborio rice

2 eggs, hard boiled

120 g/4 oz/½ cup cooked ham, sliced about ½ cm/¼ in thick

75 g/3 oz/½ cup hard cheese such as Gruyère or Fontina, diced

1 medium frankfurter sausage, diced

10 black olives, pitted and diced

½ red bell pepper, diced

½ yellow bell pepper, diced

3 tbsp sweetcorn kernels

2 tbsp salt-preserved capers, rinsed

1 tbsp small pickled onions

juice of 1 large lemon

3 tbsp extra virgin olive oil

15–20 fresh basil leaves

salt and pepper

My Secret

Unlike most Italian rice dishes, in this recipe the rice must be rinsed after cooking, so that the grains do not stick together.

Insalata di Riso is nicer if made a few hours in advance.

Insalata di Carciofi e Grana

Raw artichoke salad with Parmesan cheese

Serves 4

60 g/2 oz/¼–½ cup piece
Grana Padano cheese

8 baby artichokes

2 lemons, halved

3 tbsp extra virgin olive oil

salt and freshly ground
pepper

The best artichokes for this recipe are the baby ones which are harvested in winter or early spring. This salad is delicious and is best served as a starter.

Cut the cheese into flakes using a potato peeler then set aside.

Prepare the artichokes one at a time. Cut off and discard the stem and the top. Working all the way round the artichokes, peel off the tough outer leaves. Rub each artichoke with the cut side of a lemon half and squeeze some juice down into the centre. Place the artichokes in a bowl of cold water that you have flavoured with some of the juice from the lemons.

When you are ready to serve the salad, drain the artichokes and dry them. With a sharp knife, cut each in half lengthways and continue slicing them lengthways into wafer-thin slices.

Place the artichoke slices in a salad bowl. Dress them with the extra virgin olive oil, a few drops of lemon juice, and some salt and pepper. Toss gently, then sprinkle the cheese flakes on top and serve.

My Secrets

To avoid staining your hands, try wearing rubber gloves while handling the artichokes.

The lemon helps prevent the artichokes turning dark.

Do not use large globe artichokes for this salad as they are too tough to eat raw.

Insalata di Fagioli e Cipolla

Tuscan bean salad

One of the simplest salads in Italy and yet one of the most popular, Tuscan bean salad is inevitably featured as part of a summer buffet table. Once again, it is the quality of the ingredients that will make all the difference.

Slice the onion into rings, then separate the rings and leave them to soak in a bowl of chilled, salted water for at least 30 minutes.

Meanwhile, in a small saucepan, hard boil the eggs. Leave them to cool, then peel and set aside.

Rinse the beans under hot water, then drain and set aside. Drain the tuna and use a fork to break it roughly into chunks.

When the onion has been soaking for 30 minutes, drain it thoroughly. In a large bowl, combine the onion rings, canellini beans and tuna and toss gently.

Add the olive oil and vinegar and season the salad with salt and pepper. Sprinkle with the parsley. Halve the eggs and use them to decorate the salad, then serve.

Serves 4

1 large red onion

2 eggs

1 x 240 g/8 oz can canellini beans

180 g/6 oz canned Mediterranean tuna in olive oil

2 tbsp extra virgin olive oil

1 tsp very strong red wine vinegar

salt and freshly ground black pepper

1 tsp parsley, chopped

My Secrets

Soaking the sliced onion in salt water takes away the strong taste, leaving it crunchy and sweet. Put this secret to work whenever you use raw onions!

When peeling hard-boiled eggs, do it under running water. The skin will come off a lot more easily.

The best tuna for this salad is Italian or Spanish. Skipjack tuna is too dry and stringy.

Insalata Caprese
Capri salad

Serves 6

1 tbsp salt-preserved capers

6 medium tomatoes, rich and ripe

300 g/10 oz/1½ cups fresh Italian mozzarella

1 tsp dried oregano

6 large basil leaves

4 tbsp extra virgin olive oil

salt and pepper

There are many innovative versions of this salad, with ingredients such as avocado. They may be pleasant, but they are certainly not authentic! This recipe is a real classic of Italian cuisine and the ideal dish to serve for a summer buffet lunch.

Rinse the capers under running water until all the salt is removed.

Wash and dry the tomatoes and slice them into 0.5 cm/¼ in slices. Slice the mozzarella the same way. Arrange them on a large flat platter, alternating the tomato and cheese and slightly overlapping the slices. Sprinkle the capers and oregano on top.

Tear the basil leaves by hand and scatter them on the platter. Drizzle the salad with the olive oil and season to taste with salt and freshly ground pepper.

My Secrets

This salad is best made at the last minute, so that the tomatoes retain their moisture and texture.

Only using the best ingredients will make it a success.

Insalata Tricolore

Saffron pasta salad

My niece, Francesca, gave me the recipe for this pretty salad which makes a great impact on the table because of its colour. It tastes delicious and is an ideal summer dish served as a starter. When making a pasta salad, use a small pasta shape such as pennette or small shells. The other ingredients in the salad will make a good balance with the pasta, not only in taste, but also in size. For the method of cooking pasta for salads, see the introduction for the Pasta chapter on page 28.

In a saucepan, heat the olive oil and sauté the onion until it is translucent but not brown. Add the petits pois and 3 tablespoons of water and cook, covered, over a medium heat for 10–15 minutes, or until the peas are tender.

Add the prawns (shrimp) and chilli, season to taste with salt and pepper and turn off the heat. Set the mixture aside to cool.

Bring a large pot of salted water to the boil. Add the saffron and pasta and cook until the pasta is al dente.

Drain the pasta thoroughly, then combine it with the mixture of peas and prawns (shrimp) and serve.

Serves 6

4 tbsp extra virgin olive oil

½ onion, chopped

300 g/10 oz/1½ cups petits pois or spring peas

300 g/10 oz/1½ cups cooked prawns (shrimp), shelled

1 tsp crushed dried chilli

salt and pepper

⅛ tsp powdered saffron, or 1 tsp saffron strands

300 g/10 oz/1½ cups small dried pasta such as pennette

My Secret
Pasta salads lose a lot of their fragrant taste if refrigerated. When you wish to prepare this dish in advance, cook the peas and prawns (shrimp) beforehand, but boil the pasta at the last minute. The difference is quite remarkable.

Baking cakes and pastries

Every time my mother baked a cake, my father would say: 'This time it came out particularly well!' She was very good at baking: she made no fuss, and everything always came out perfectly, so I learned many of my secrets from her.

When you start mixing the ingredients (thank goodness for food processors! – my mother didn't have one) they should all be at room or perhaps body temperature. A significant change in the temperature of the mixture will prevent a cake from rising, or could make it sink halfway through the cooking time.

When measuring baking powder, the best approach is to follow the manufacturer's instructions, as different brands react in different ways. In Italy, baking powder is sold in sachets, each with enough powder to rise a medium-sized cake. Its quality makes a big difference to the result. Some Italian delicatessens carry it, so if you come across it, stock up.

It is most important that cakes be treated gently, and control of the oven temperature is of paramount importance. Never open the door of the oven while the cake is baking. A brisk change in temperature can stop the rising process with disastrous results. Furthermore, never slam the door of the oven after putting in the cake. Such an abrupt jar is like a slap in the face and the cake may not rise, leaving you with a heavy and unfortunate result.

Another tip is not to take the cake out of the oven when it is done. Just turn the oven off and leave the cake inside, with the door slightly open. This gives a gentle temperature change that will not threaten the lightness of your cake.

With shortcrust pastry, everything is a lot easier. It is mainly a matter of mixing the ingredients and letting them rest for a while. This is required to prevent the pastry from shrinking away from the side of the tin.

I have found it particularly effective to roll out the pastry, press it into the tin, and then let it rest in the fridge. When you consider that shortcrust pastry has a high butter content, this makes sense. The butter gets cold as the dough rests in the fridge, and therefore the pastry becomes more difficult to roll. If you roll it when it is just made and then let it rest in the fridge, the best results are achieved with much less effort.

La Mia Torta al Cioccolato

My chocolate cake

I also call this cake '4 x 4' as it needs the eggs plus the same weight of 4 other ingredients. You can use as many eggs as you want, but the proportions are always the same. It is a very simple recipe, and one that always gives good results. The cake freezes beautifully. Because of the high proportion of butter, it should not be served chilled, as the texture would be too heavy.

Preheat the oven to 180°C/350°F/Gas 4. Thoroughly butter a 22 cm/9 in springform tin and coat it with flour, knocking out the excess. Weigh the eggs in their shells and measure out the same weight of sugar, butter, dark chocolate and flour.

Using an electric mixer, beat the eggs with the sugar until the mixture is pale and fluffy, about 8 minutes.

Add the softened butter and melted chocolate and keep beating until smooth. Remove the bowl from the mixer and fold in the sifted flour, then pour the mixture into the prepared tin.

Bake for about 45 minutes. Towards the end of cooking it may be necessary to cover the top of the cake with foil to prevent the surface from burning. Serve at room temperature, with cream.

Serves 6

4 eggs

the same weight of caster (superfine) sugar

the same weight of butter, softened, plus extra for greasing

the same weight of dark (semi-sweet) chocolate, melted

the same weight of plain (all-purpose) white flour, sifted, plus extra for dusting

My Secrets

This cake is very easy to do because it doesn't require any baking powder. The only way to make it come out well is to incorporate as much air as possible into the mix. This is done during the whisking phase, so don't be afraid of over-whisking it.

To check it is cooked, insert a knife or a stick near the edge; it should come out dry, while the stick should still be wet coming out of the centre of the cake. It is important that the centre of the cake is still sticky, to be really delicious.

Pan Meino
Polenta cake

Serves 6

100 g/3½ oz/½ cup butter, plus extra for greasing

120 g/4 oz/½ cup caster (superfine) sugar

2 large eggs, separated

3 drops vanilla essence

100 g/3½ oz/½ cup plain (all-purpose) white flour

100 g/3½ oz/½ cup maize flour or cornmeal, plus extra for dusting

15 g/½ oz/1½ tbsp baking powder, or one packet Italian baking powder

150 ml/5 fl oz/⅔ cup whole milk

A delicious Milanese speciality that is rather dry so it should be served with lots of single (light) cream. It is also ideal with morning tea, coffee or cappuccino.

Preheat the oven to 180°C/350°F/Gas 4. Grease a round 20 cm/8 in cake tin with butter and dust with maize flour.

In a large bowl, combine the butter with all but 1 tablespoon of the sugar and mix until fluffy. Add the egg yolks and vanilla essence. Mix the plain flour and maize flour with the baking powder and add to the mixture with the milk.

Beat the egg whites until firm then fold the egg whites into the cake mixture.

Pour the cake mixture into the prepared cake tin and sprinkle the top with the remaining sugar. Bake for about 50 minutes. Serve with single cream.

My Secret
This is a very simple recipe. Following the directions about baking in the introduction will ensure that you are successful!

Torta di Riso
Sweet rice cake

This is my aunt's recipe and one that is very dear to me. She would always make it for my uncle's birthday. I have never found it in an Italian cookery book. What I like about it is the contrast between the smoothness of the rice and the crunchiness of the almonds and candied lemon peel.

Preheat the oven to 180°C/350°F/Gas 4. Generously butter a deep rectangular ovenproof dish about 30 cm/12 in long and 5 cm/2 in deep. Dust the dish with the breadcrumbs and tap out the excess.

Bring the milk to a boil, add the rice, and cook over a low heat for 30–40 minutes or until all the milk is absorbed. Add the caster (superfine) sugar, stir and leave to cool.

Add the eggs, almonds, candied peel and lemon zest to the rice and stir gently. Add the liquor.

Pour the mixture into the prepared dish and bake for about 1 hour. Remove from the oven and leave to cool.

To serve, cut the cooled cake into 5 cm/2 in squares and sprinkle with icing (confectioner's) sugar. Serve chilled with a cocktail stick in each piece.

Makes 24 squares

butter, for greasing

fine breadcrumbs, for dusting

1 litre/2 pints/5 cups whole milk

120 g/4 oz/½ cup arborio rice

210 g/7 oz/1 cup caster (superfine) sugar

6 medium eggs, beaten

120 g/4 oz/½ cup toasted almonds, chopped

120 g/4 oz/½ cup candied lemon peel

grated zest of 1 large lemon

4 tbsp of cognac or dark rum (optional)

icing (confectioner's) sugar, sifted, to decorate

My Secrets
When cooking rice in milk, use a heavy pot to ensure even heating. Make sure that the heat is very low, and that you stir from time to time while the rice is cooking. Milk tends to stick to the bottom of the pan, particularly when mixed with something as starchy as rice.

When grating the lemon, make sure you grate only the yellow zest and not down to the white of the lemon rind, which would give a bitter taste to the cake.

Torta di Mele di Marina

Marina's apple cake

Serves 6–8

fine breadcrumbs or flour, for dusting

175 g/6 oz/¾ cup sultanas

120 ml/4 fl oz/½ cup dark rum

7 medium eating apples, such as Granny Smith or Golden Delicious

120 ml/4 fl oz/½ cup sweet white wine, sherry or calvados

juice of 1 lemon

8 tbsp caster (superfine) sugar

100 g/3½ oz/½ cup butter, preferably unsalted, at room temperature, plus extra for greasing

2 medium eggs

100 g/3½ oz/½ cup plain (all-purpose) white flour

1 tsp baking powder

Marina, one of my dearest friends, gave me this recipe, which is a nice alternative to the usual apple pie. Unusually, the apples are combined with the cake mix and everything is cooked together. The outcome is moist and delicate and looks very pretty. It is ideal served warm with ice-cream or cream.

Grease a 20 cm/8 in springform cake tin with butter then dust with some breadcrumbs or flour and tap out the excess. In a small bowl, soak the sultanas in the rum.

Peel the apples and slice them very thinly, preferably using a food processor or a mandoline. Marinate the apple slices for at least 1 hour in the wine, lemon juice and 5 tablespoons of the sugar, stirring occasionally to make sure that all the apples are covered with the juices.

In a mixing bowl, with an electric whisk, whip the butter with the remaining 5 tablespoons of sugar. Add the eggs, flour and then the baking powder and whisk until very fluffy.

Preheat the oven to 180°C/350°F/Gas 4. Drain the apples and the sultanas, discarding the liquids in which they were soaking. Fold the fruit into the cake mixture.

Pour the cake mixture into the prepared cake tin and spread out to fill the dish. Bake for 1½ hours.

My Secret
Whip the butter with the other ingredients until everything is really nice and fluffy before adding the apples. When making a cake, encourage lots of air into the mix. Your final result will be light and delicate because of the air that is trapped inside.

Torta al Cioccolato con le Pere

Chocolate and pear torte

The combination of chocolate and pears is really delicious. This recipe came from Giuditta and is good example of Italian family cooking. It is simple and looks pretty but not manicured.

Grease a 23 cm/9 in springform tin and dust with flour. Preheat the oven to 180°C/350°F/Gas4.

Peel and core the pears and cut them into segments 1 cm/½ in thick. Set aside.

In a mixing bowl, beat the butter and sugar together until pale and fluffy. Add the egg yolks and continue beating until fluffy. Add the lemon juice.

Mix together the flour, cocoa powder and baking powder and add them to the egg mixture. Beat the milk into the flour mix to ease the mixing.

In a large bowl, beat the egg whites until firm. Fold them gently into the cake mixture.

Pour the cake mixture into the prepared cake tin. Push the pear segments into the mixture in a circle.

Bake for 1 hour 15 minutes, or until a knife inserted in the cake comes out clean. Remove the cake from the tin (do not turn it over). Dust with icing sugar and serve while still warm with ice-cream or double (heavy) cream.

Serves 6–8

500 g/1 lb/2½ cups pears, firm textured

150 g/5 oz/¾ cup salted butter, plus extra for greasing

150 g/5 oz/¾ cup caster (superfine) sugar

4 large eggs, separated

1 tbsp lemon juice

240 g/8 oz/1½ cups plain (all-purpose) white flour, plus extra for dusting

2 tbsp unsweetened cocoa powder

15 g/½ oz/1½ tbsp baking powder, or one packet Italian baking powder

2 tbsp whole milk, at room temperature

icing (confectioner's) sugar, sifted, to decorate

My Secrets

If the tin you choose is larger than the size suggested, the cake may take a little less time to cook as it will be thinner.

The pears you use should be firm and not too ripe as they need to keep their shape. If too ripe and juicy they may turn mushy.

Rotolo di Meringa con Marron Glasse'

Meringue roulade with chestnut and cream filling

Serves 8–10

4 large egg whites

240 g/8 oz/1¼ cup caster (superfine) sugar

1 tbsp cornflour (cornstarch)

1 tbsp lemon juice

100 g/3½ oz/½ cup toasted hazelnuts, chopped

vegetable oil, for greasing

icing (confectioner's) sugar, sifted, for dusting

For the filling:

300 ml/10 fl oz/1¼ cups whipping (light whipping) cream

360 g/12 oz/1¾ cups marrons glacé, or fruit in season, to taste

Ultrasweet meringue combined with delicate and delicious chestnuts: this dish is perfect for making a big impression, especially when served with a chocolate sauce.

Using an electric mixer, beat the egg whites to soft peaks. With the mixer still running, gradually add the sugar and cornflour (cornstarch). Add the lemon juice and continue until the mixture is very stiff with glossy peaks. Fold in the chopped hazelnuts, then set aside.

Preheat the oven to 150°C/300°F/Gas 2. Line a baking sheet with a piece of parchment paper and brush the paper with the vegetable oil. Using a spatula, spread the meringue mixture evenly over the sheet. Bake for 30–40 minutes or until the top is pale golden brown and the centre is still soft. Set aside to cool.

To prepare the filling, whip the cream to stiff peaks. Reserve a few whole marrons glacé for decoration and chop the remainder. Mix the chopped marrons glacé into the cream and then spread the cream mixture on top of the meringue.

Run a long, sharp knife between the meringue and the parchment paper to loosen the meringue. Roll it up into a cylinder, tightly but gently, using the parchment paper to help curve it round.

When ready to serve, dust the roulade with icing (confectioner's) sugar and decorate with the reserved whole marrons glacé. Serve in slices.

My Secrets

Since every oven behaves differently, the best way to check that the meringue is done is to touch it in the centre. It should be crisp on top, but still soft inside, a bit like a sponge.

Roll the meringue up from the long side of the baking sheet. Rolling from the short side will make the roulade too large in diameter.

A good way to measure the proportion between egg white and sugar is to double the weight of sugar to the egg white.

Rotolo di Cioccolata e Castagne

Chocolate roulade with chestnut and ricotta filling

The perfect ending to a meal for the festive season, the practical advantage of this dish is that you can prepare it in advance, and it freezes well. Take heart: it's also easier to make than it seems!

To make the biscuit, use an electric mixer to beat the egg yolks and sugar together in a large bowl for about 5 minutes until the mixture is thick and pale and forms a ribbon when the beater is lifted. Add the cocoa powder and keep beating a little more to mix. Set aside.

Heat the oven to 180°C/350°F/Gas 4. Line a baking tray with a large sheet of parchment paper and brush it with vegetable oil.

In a separate large bowl, whisk the egg whites until they form stiff peaks. Fold them into the yolk mixture and spread evenly over the paper, smooth over the surface, and bake for 20–25 minutes. Leave to cool before rolling.

To prepare the filling, pass the chestnut purée through a mouli-légumes or a sieve into a bowl. Add the ricotta cheese and mix well to a nice creamy texture, then add the vanilla and icing (confectioner's) sugar to taste.

Dust a new sheet of parchment paper with icing sugar. When the biscuit is cold, turn it over onto the new sheet of parchment. Mix the rum with 4 tablespoons of water and brush the mixture over the biscuit. Spread the chestnut filling on top.

Working from the long side, roll up into a cylinder using the parchment sheet to help curve it round. Wrap the roulade tightly in foil and refrigerate. When ready to serve, dust the roulade with more icing sugar and trim off the ends to give a neat finish. (Eat the scraps to reward yourself!)

Serves 8

For the biscuit:

6 large eggs, separated

150 g/6 oz/¾ cup caster (superfine) sugar

60 g/2 oz/¼–½ cup unsweetened cocoa powder

vegetable oil, for greasing

icing (confectioner's) sugar, for dusting

4 tbsp rum

For the filling:

1 x 250 g/9 oz tin unsweetened chestnut purée

250 g/9 oz/1¼ cups ricotta cheese

a few drops of vanilla extract

6 tbsp icing (confectioner's) sugar

marrons glacé, for decoration

My Secret

Like the meringue roulade, the daunting part of this recipe is the rolling. Lift one side of the parchment paper to help you ease the mixture over into a cylinder. It will be really easy!

Zuccotto al Marsala

Home-made ice cream in a sponge shell

Serves 8

For the sponge:

4 medium eggs

150 g/5 oz/¾ cup caster (superfine) sugar

a few drops of vanilla extract, or the grated zest of 1 lemon

150 g/5 oz/¾ cup plain (all-purpose) white flour, plus extra for dusting

For the filling:

400 ml/13 fl oz/1½ cups whipping (light whipping) cream

60 g/2 oz/¼–½ cup icing (confectioner's) sugar

120 g/4 oz/¾ cup dark (semi-sweet) chocolate chips, or grated chocolate

120 g/4 oz/½ cup mixed candied peel

120 ml/4 fl oz/½ cup marsala wine, plus 1 tbsp

One of the oldest Italian traditions, Zuccotto is a classic pudding that has great impact at the table. It is basically ice-cream served in a sponge shell soaked with liquor and there are several versions. In Sicily they add candied peel and chocolate chips; in Piedmont they add hazelnuts. Try it with fresh berries in summer or candied chestnuts in autumn.

Grease a 22 cm/9 in springform tin and dust it with flour, tapping out the excess. Preheat the oven to 180°C/350°F/Gas 4.

To make the sponge, beat the eggs and sugar in an electric mixer at maximum speed for 15 minutes or until very fluffy and pale. Add the vanilla extract or lemon zest.

Sift the flour onto the egg mixture and quickly fold it in with a large spatula. When all the flour has been absorbed, pour the mixture into the prepared tin and bake for 35–40 minutes. Remove to a rack to cool slowly.

To make the filling, whip the cream and icing (confectioner's) sugar together until fluffy. Add the chocolate, candied peel and 1 tablespoon of marsala and place in the fridge to chill.

Line a round bowl of 1.5 litre/2½ pint/7 cup capacity with a large sheet of cling film. Cut the sponge into 1 cm/½ in slices and use them to line the bowl. Combine the 120 ml /4 floz/½ cup of marsala with an equal quantity of water and brush the mixture liberally over the sponge.

Pour the whipped cream mixture into the centre of the bowl and knock the bowl gently on the counter top to make sure that there are no air bubbles. Top with a lid of sponge slices soaked in marsala and freeze for at least 3 hours.

Place the pudding in the fridge for 1–1½ hours before serving.

My Secrets

This recipe can be made in stages. The sponge, for example, can be made in advance and frozen.

Be sure to whip the eggs and sugar for the sponge until very fluffy and foamy. As there isn't any baking powder in this sponge, the raising agent is the air trapped in the egg mixture and there must be plenty of it to make the sponge light.

Home-made Ice Cream in a Sponge Shell (page 128)

Aubergine Rolls with Parma Ham (page 105) and Grilled Bell Peppers (page 104)

Potato Cake with Almonds (page 109) and Tomato Sauce (page 43)

Torta di Ricotta

Ricotta tart

This is the 'Italian Cheesecake', which doesn't have much to do with its American cousin. Do not try to make it with cream cheese if you don't have any ricotta available. The final result would be good, but with the ricotta, it will be outstanding!

To make the pastry, place all the ingredients in a food processor and blend until the dough comes together. If you choose to make the pastry by hand, try to work quickly so that the pastry is not heated by your hands.

Roll out the pastry and press it into the base and sides of a 22 cm/ 9 in pie dish – do not worry if it crumbles and breaks, you can repair it with your hands with no harm to the final result. Place in the bottom of the fridge to rest for about 1 hour.

Preheat the oven to 180°C/350°F/Gas 4. To prepare the filling, mix the ricotta cheese, eggs, sugar, cream and lemon zest, using an electric whisk if desired. The filling should be as thick as double (heavy) cream.

Pour the filling into the chilled pastry case and bake for about 45 minutes. Leave the cheesecake to cool and then chill until ready to serve.

Serves 6

For the pastry:

120 g/4 oz/½ cup plain (all-purpose) flour

120 g/4 oz/½ cup unsalted butter, at room temperature

5 tbsp caster (superfine) sugar

grated zest of 1 lemon

1 egg yolk

For the filling:

500 g/1 lb/2½ cups ricotta cheese

2 whole eggs

5 tbsp caster (superfine) sugar

3 tbsp single (light) cream

grated zest of 1 lemon

My Secret

Handling pastry is always a messy job. My solution is to cut a large sheet of parchment paper and place it on the work top. When the dough is made, tip it onto the paper and use the paper to shape the pastry into a ball: you touch the pastry with the paper rather than your hands, so it does not stick to your hands or the worktop. Then take a second sheet of parchment paper, place it on top of the pastry, and roll out the pastry over the second sheet of paper so that the paper forms a pastry sandwich. This gives you a thin layer of pastry ready to transfer to the tin with no mess and no wasted pastry! Rest this 'sandwich' in the fridge until the butter has become really hard.

Crema Pasticcera
Plain custard for fillings

For a small tart, about
20 cm/8 in diameter.

250 ml/9 fl oz/1¼ cups
whole milk

2 egg yolks

1 tbsp plain (all-purpose)
white flour

5 tbsp caster (superfine)
sugar

1 tsp vanilla extract, or
grated zest of 1 lemon, or
4 tbsp liquor, such as rum
or marsala, or 60 g/2 oz/
¼ cup dark (semi-sweet)
chocolate pieces

This custard is ideal to fill a sponge or tart and can be eaten with
cookies. If you have an ice cream maker you can make delicious
ice cream with it too. The flavour can be changed according to your
taste: vanilla, lemon, chocolate... as you like.

Bring the milk to the boil, then set aside. Meanwhile, in a stainless
steel bowl, beat the egg yolks, flour and sugar until the mixture has
doubled in volume and is very fluffy and pale. Add the vanilla extract,
or lemon zest.

Slowly add the hot milk, stirring constantly over a low heat.

Simmer gently until you feel that the sauce is starting to thicken.
Cook for at least 10 minutes once the custard starts to thicken.

If you are making the chocolate version, grate the chocolate finely
and add it to the cooked hot sauce, stirring until the chocolate has
completely melted. The same applies if you are using liquor. Add it to
the custard when it is completely cooked.

My Secrets
Patience is the secret of this sauce. As you start adding the milk,
the custard looks very liquid and it will take a while before it starts
thickening. Do not give up stirring, as you'll see that all of a sudden
the custard thickens and if you stop stirring, lumps will appear.
At this point, keep cooking the custard for at least 10 minutes to get
rid of the taste of uncooked flour.

As this custard tends to stick to the bottom of the pan, be careful
and keep the heat very low indeed.

Crostata di Frutta

Pastry base for fruit tart

Here is a basic pastry recipe that can be used for virtually any sweet tart. When I moved to England, I couldn't understand what 'baking blind' meant. I now know that it means baking 'empty' or with no filling, but I still don't know what blindness has to do with this method. The technique is not difficult, but it does require attention.

In a food processor, mix all the ingredients until they form a compact ball. Remove the dough from the processor, wrap it in cling film and put in the fridge to rest for at least 30 minutes.

Line a 25 cm/10 in tart dish or tin with the pastry to a depth of 1 cm/⅛ in. Ensure that the sides of the pastry dish are carefully covered as they will hold the custard.

Preheat the oven to 180°C/350°F/Gas 4. Prick the base of the pastry case with a fork and then cover it with a large sheet of baking parchment and some baking beans. Bake for about 10 minutes or until the pastry is a pale gold.

Remove the beans from the pastry case by lifting up the paper and return the tart case to the oven for another 6–10 minutes – after which it will still be a little soft.

Set the pastry case aside to cool and harden, then fill with Crema Pasticcera (Plain custard, see opposite) and decorate with fruits of your choice, such as apricots, grapes or strawberries. Dust the filled and decorated tart with icing sugar just before going to the table.

Makes 1 x 25 cm/10 in tart

500 g/1 lb/2½ cups plain (all-purpose) white flour

210 g/7 oz/1 cup butter

210 g/7 oz/1 cup caster (superfine) sugar

2 whole eggs plus 1 yolk extra

1 tsp baking powder

dried beans or clean pebbles for baking

icing (confectioner's) sugar, sifted, to decorate

My Secrets

The weight of the beans prevents the pastry from rising while cooking. The parchment paper is necessary to remove the beans from the base – allow enough extra paper to sit up over the rim so that you can take hold of it and lift the beans out easily.

Some pastry bases are very crisp but hard to cut. This one is deliciously short and light. The secret is in the baking powder and the cooking time. Never overcook your base: only the sides should be coloured like a biscuit. If you cook the pastry until it is brown all over it will be too hard once cool.

Torta al Cioccolato Senza Farina

Wheat-free chocolate torte

Serves 10–12

360 g/12 oz/2¼ cups dark (semi-sweet) chocolate, chopped

170 g/6 oz/1½ cup, plus 3 tbsp, unsalted butter, cut into pieces

6 large eggs, separated

12 tbsp caster (superfine) sugar

2 tsp vanilla extract

salt

Nowadays, it is increasingly common to come across people who have a wheat allergy. There are very few good recipes without flour and this is an extraordinarily good one!

Preheat the oven to 180°C/350°F/Gas 4. Line a 22 cm/9 in diameter springform cake tin with baking parchment.

Stir the chocolate and butter together in a heavy-based saucepan over a low heat until melted and smooth. Remove from the heat and leave to cool, stirring frequently. Using an electric whisk, beat the egg yolks and 6 tbsp sugar in a large bowl until the mixture is very thick and pale.

Fold the lukewarm chocolate mixture into the yolk mixture, then fold in the vanilla extract.

Beat the egg whites with a pinch of salt in another large bowl until soft peaks form. Gradually add the remaining sugar and continue beating until medium-firm peaks form.

Using a large spoon or spatula, gently fold the whites into the chocolate mixture a little at a time. Pour the mixture into the prepared tin.

Bake the cake for about 50 minutes until the top is puffed and cracked. A skewer inserted into the centre should come out with moist crumbs attached.

My Secret
The secret for this recipe lies in the quality of the chocolate you use. I suggest one with a cocoa content of at least 53 per cent, preferably 70 per cent. This will be stated on the packaging.

Torta di Amaretti

Amaretto Torte

This torte is quite rustic and moist and is ideal with afternoon tea. The combination of ground almonds and amaretti biscuits makes it rich.

Using an electric whisk, beat together the sugar, butter and vanilla extract until very fluffy. Add the yolks, one at a time, beating continuously.

Add the breadcrumbs, crushed amaretti biscuits and ground almonds. Beat the egg whites to soft peaks, then fold them gently into the mixture.

Pour the mixture into a 20–23 cm/8½–9 in springform tin, previously lined with baking parchment. Bake in a preheated oven at 180°C/350°F/Gas 4 for 35–40 minutes.

Serves 8–10

200 g/7 oz/1 cup caster (superfine) sugar

200 g/7 oz/1 cup unsalted butter, at room temperature

1 tsp vanilla extract

6 large eggs, separated

2 tsp home-made breadcrumbs

200 g/7 oz/1 cup ground amaretti biscuits

150 g/5 oz/¾ cup ground almonds

pinch salt

My Secret

To make sure that this torte comes out perfectly, make your own breadcrumbs from any white, leftover bread. Dry the bread completely in the oven at low temperature then, when it has cooled, place it in a food processor and process until all the bread is very fine, like sand. Before using the breadcrumbs to make the torte, sieve them to remove any large pieces. Breadcrumbs keep for weeks in an airtight container, and are indispensable for several Italian recipes.

Crostata di Uvetta e Pinoli

Sultana and pine nut tart

Serves 6–8

120 g/4 oz/½–¾ cup
sultanas

rum or cognac, for soaking

60 g/2 oz/¼–½ cup pine
nuts

For the pastry:

300 g/10 oz/1½ cups plain
(all-purpose) white flour

120 g/4 oz/½–¾ cup
unsalted butter

60 g/2 oz/¼–½ cup icing
(confectioner's) sugar

1 egg

For the custard:

5 egg yolks

150 g/5 oz/¾ cup caster
(superfine) sugar

240 ml/8 fl oz/1 cup single
(light) cream

a few drops of vanilla
extract

icing (confectioner's)
sugar, sifted, for decoration

*One of my favourite tarts, this should not be served right out of the
oven as the custard might be too runny. It is best when made some
hours in advance. The method for lining the pastry tin is the same as
in Torte di Ricotte (Ricotta tart), page 129.*

Place the sultanas in a small bowl and add rum or cognac to cover.
Leave to soak for several hours.

To make the pastry, in a food processor mix together all the
ingredients to form a dough. Line a 23 cm/9 in dish with the pastry,
making sure that the sides are carefully covered and the edge is
1.5 cm/¾ in high. Set aside to rest in a cool place for at least 1 hour.

Preheat the oven to 180°C/350°F/Gas 4. To make the custard, in a
bowl beat the egg yolks with the sugar until the sugar is completely
dissolved. Stir in the cream and vanilla extract and set aside.

Drain the sultanas. Scatter them and the pine nuts over the base of
the uncooked pastry case, then pour in the custard.

Bake for about 45 minutes or until the sides of the tart look golden.
Leave the tart to cool and sprinkle with sifted icing (confectioner's)
sugar before serving.

My Secrets

To give an attractive scalloped edge to the pastry, use the back of a
spoon or a fork to gently press down on the dough around the rim.

The egg whites left over from making the custard can be frozen and
used for the meringue roulade on page 104.

If you have some pastry left over, shape into a cylinder with about a
5 cm/2 in diameter and chill. When you are ready, cut the pastry into
little wheels 1 cm/⅛ in thick and make delicious biscuits. Alternative,
freeze the left over pastry.

Ovis Molis

Classic Italian cookies

Hard-boiled eggs are the unusual base for these extraordinarily delicate cookies. They are delicious served with tea or coffee.

In a small saucepan, boil the eggs for 10 minutes until hard. Cool under running water and peel. Discard the white and sieve the yolks into a mixing bowl.

Sift the flour and sugar into the mixing bowl, then add the softened butter and vanilla extract. Start mixing with an electric whisk, then add the milk.

When everything is thoroughly combined, tip the dough out onto a sheet of parchment paper and roll it into logs about 2.5 cm/1 in in diameter. Leave to rest in the fridge for 30 minutes.

Preheat the oven to 180°C/350°F/Gas 4 and line a baking (cookie) sheet with parchment paper. Cut the chilled logs into walnut-sized pieces and use your hands to roll them into small balls.

Place the balls on the baking sheet and use your thumb to make an indentation in the centre of each ball. Use a teaspoon to fill the holes with a little jam. Bake for 10–15 minutes or until light golden.

Makes 28–30

3 eggs

150 g/5 oz/¾ cup plain flour

90 g/3 oz/¼–½ cup caster (superfine) sugar

4 tbsp butter, softened

2 drops vanilla extract

2 tbsp whole milk

3–4 tbsp apricot jam

My Secret
To prevent them from cracking while boiling, eggs should be at room temperature before being placed in the water. Rinsing them under cold water when cooked will prevent a black ring from forming around the yolk.

Amaretti Morbidi

Soft amaretti

Makes 30–35

240 g/9 oz/1¼ cups
blanched almonds

240 g/9 oz/1 heaping cup
caster (superfine) sugar

1 egg white

1 tbsp single (light) cream

a few drops of almond
essence

icing (confectioner's)
sugar, for dusting

*These Amaretti are the first thing I sold when I started my cookery
school: I was making them to serve with coffee and they were so
popular that people wanted to buy them. They are not difficult to
make, but if you don't bake them properly they will turn as hard
as a rock.*

Heat the oven to 180°C/350°F/Gas 4. Place the almonds on a baking
sheet and toast them for about 10 minutes. Leave the oven on to
bake the Amaretti later.

Cool, then grind the almonds in a food processor with the sugar until
very fine indeed.

Add the egg white, cream and almond essence and mix thoroughly,
first with a spoon and then with your hands.

Line a baking (cookie) sheet with parchment paper. Shape the
almond mixture into balls the size of a small apricot and place them
on the parchment paper 1 cm/½ in apart. Bake for 6–10 minutes until
the Amaretti start to colour.

Leave the biscuits to cool, then dust them with icing (confectioner's)
sugar and eat. They can be stored in an airtight tin for a few days.

My Secrets

You can avoid the first step of grinding the almonds by using almond
flour, but make sure that it is fresh, otherwise the Amaretti will have a
stale taste.

The cooking time varies with each oven. The best way to make sure
that the cooking time is right is to bake the amaretti for 5 minutes
and then check their colour every 2 minutes. They are done when
they turn a very light beige.

Biscottini di Polenta

Home-made polenta cookies

This is a recipe from the north of Italy. The original name of the cookies is 'zaleti' and they are delicious dipped in espresso.

In a bowl, beat the egg yolks and caster (superfine) sugar until pale and fluffy. Meanwhile, in a small pan, melt the butter gently.

Sift the plain (all-purpose) flour, maize flour (cornmeal) and baking powder over the yolk mixture. Beat in the melted butter and then, using a wooden spoon, stir in the sultanas and mix well.

Shape the mixture into 2 cylinders about 5 cm/2 in in diameter. Wrap in parchment paper and leave to rest in the fridge until the rolls harden.

Line a baking (cookie) sheet with parchment paper and preheat the oven to 180°C/350°F/Gas 4. Cut the chilled rolls into discs 1 cm/½ in thick. Lay them on the baking (cookie) sheet and bake for 15 minutes or until they are just light golden but still soft in the centre.

Leave the cookies to cool and dust them with icing (confectioner's) sugar before serving. They will keep in an airtight tin for several days.

Makes 48

3 egg yolks

100 g/3½ oz/½ cup caster (superfine) sugar

150 g/5 oz/¾ cup butter, melted

150 g/5 oz/¾ cup plain (all-purpose) white flour

150 g/5 oz/¾ cup maize flour (cornmeal)

½ tsp baking powder

100 g/3½ oz/½ cup sultanas, soaked in hot water

icing (confectioner's) sugar, sifted, for decoration

My Secrets

When shaping the dough into rolls, there is no need to touch the dough as you can tip it from the bowl directly onto the paper that wraps it. Use the paper to protect your hands while you roll the dough into cylinders. It's easier than it sounds!

Do not lay the cookies too close to each other on the baking sheet as they will expand while cooking.

The centre of the cookies will still be soft to the touch at the end of the cooking time; be careful not to overcook them. All cookies harden when they cool.

Desserts

Desserts for special occasions

Only on special or festive occasions does a traditional Italian meal end with a dessert or cake. Usually, it is fruit that ends our meals. However, there are some extraordinary desserts that are truly Italian. I have chosen a selection of the most popular ones, which are always a success.

In Italy we love sweets, but rich desserts are rarely served at home: cheese and fruit end a typical meal. One reason for this must be the wonderful selection of local seasonal fruits available on the market.

Decorated cakes and elaborate confections are usually bought, rather than made at home, and are served at parties or special celebrations. It is very common in Italy to see whole families walking out of church after Sunday mass, then strolling towards the nearest bar pasticceria. There, the adults enjoy an espresso or aperitif, while the children have a fruit juice. Then, a large tray of pasticcini or a cake is bought, as a finale for the family Sunday lunch.

These delicious pasticcini are generally mini eclairs with vanilla or chocolate custard filling, or mini meringues with wild strawberries and whipped cream. They are far too fiddly and time-consuming for mamma to make!

Alternatively, for a classic end to a meal, enjoy one of Italy's renowned panettone di Milano, panforte di Siena, cassata siciliana or pandoro di Verona – I have never come across anyone who actually makes them at home, and there is certainly no shame in buying them.

Having said all this, there are a few fantastic regional family desserts that I want to share with you. They are all very, very simple to make and my secrets will guarantee their success.

Tirami Su'

Lift me up

Tirami Su' in Italian literally means 'lift me up'. This confirms that this dessert is very rich and can lift up even the weakest or most dispirited person. Not ideal for low calorie diets! There are several different versions of Tirami Su'. The original recipe is made with mascarpone, which is a cheese that looks like very rich double cream and is readily available in most supermarkets. The perfect dish in which to serve Tirami Su' is a lasagne dish, as the Tirami Su' is done in two layers only, not like a trifle.

With an electric mixer, beat the egg yolks and sugar together for about 5 minutes or until the mixture is thick and pale and forms a ribbon when the beaters are lifted. Add the mascarpone and keep whisking. Mix in the marsala and set aside.

In a large bowl, whisk the egg whites until firm. Using a spatula, gently fold them into the mascarpone mixture.

Place the cold coffee in a shallow bowl. Dip the biscuits in the coffee then place them in the serving dish in a single layer. Pour half the mascarpone mixture on top and spread it out evenly. Place another layer of coffee-soaked biscuits on top and cover with the remaining mascarpone mixture.

Cover the dish with cling film and chill for a few hours. Before serving, dust the Tirami Su' with cocoa powder, until all the surface is darkened.

Serves 8

3 eggs, separated

3 tbsp caster (superfine) sugar

250 g/9 oz/1¼ cups mascarpone cheese

4 tbsp marsala wine

500 ml/1 pint/2½ cups espresso or other very strong coffee, cold

2 packets Savoiard biscuits or lady's fingers

unsweetened cocoa powder, for dusting

My Secret
When soaking the biscuits, make sure that only the outer part of the biscuit is soaked, and the centre is still dry. It takes just a second to over-soak the biscuits, but this ruins the final result.

Creme Caramel
Caramel pudding

Serves 6–8

180 g/67 oz/¾ cup
granulated sugar

500 ml/1 pint/2½ cups
whole milk

pared rind of 1 lemon

3 large whole eggs, plus
4 large yolks

There is no risk of disappointment with Creme Caramel. It is a definite favourite at the end of any meal. Excellent for entertaining, great when there is an extra pint of milk in the fridge, ideal for children who are fussy about drinking milk, it seems its only disadvantage is that you are left with four spare egg whites, but you can always make meringues or Amaretti with them. Egg whites also freeze very well.

To caramelize the sugar, in a small saucepan place 3 tablespoons of sugar and 2 teaspoons of water. Turn the heat on and let it cook without stirring until the sugar darkens to the colour of dark rum. Pour it immediately into a 1litre/2 pint/5 cup mould, tilting the caramel all around in order to cover the bottom of the mould. Be careful as the sugar is extremely hot!

To make the custard, in a saucepan bring the milk to the boil. Turn off the heat and add the remaining sugar and the lemon rind, stirring to dissolve the sugar. Set aside to infuse.

Meanwhile, preheat the oven to 150°C/300°F/Gas 2. When the milk is cool, discard the lemon peel. In a bowl, beat the whole eggs and yolks together with a fork. Add them to the cooled milk, stirring to combine.

Strain the custard into the mould to remove any bits of egg that did not dissolve in the milk. Bake in a bain-marie for about 1 hour – the water of the bain-marie must be simmering when it goes into the oven. Turn off the oven and leave the Creme Caramel in there to cool down.

Chill the Creme Caramel before unmoulding it and serving.

My Secrets
For a bain-marie, bring a kettle of water to the boil. Place the filled mould into the empty bain-marie container and put it into the oven, then slowly pour the boiling water into the bain-marie container. Leave the cooked custard and bain-marie to cool in the oven.

I always make Creme Caramel one day in advance because it is easier to unmould when completely cold. Before turning it out, detach the top skin of the dessert from the mould with a thin knife to prevent sticking. Hold the mould in your hands and shake it from side to side so that the dessert comes loose from the mould.

Zabaglione Ghiacciato
Iced zabaglione

Classic Zabaglione is a warm custard made with eggs, sugar and marsala wine all whipped together. It is normally served for tea on a winter afternoon. My version of Zabaglione is a delicious mousse ice cream that your guests will remember, especially when accompanied by Biscotti di Polenta (Home-made polenta cookies), see page 137.

Whip the cream to soft peaks and place in the fridge.

Choose a glass bowl which fits exactly onto a saucepan, without touching its bottom. Place some water in the bottom of the saucepan and bring it to simmering point. Meanwhile, place the egg yolks, sugar and liquor in the bowl.

Place the bowl over the pan of simmering water ensuring that the water does not touch the bowl. With an electric beater, whisk for 8–10 minutes until the mixture is very pale and fluffy and has doubled in volume.

Prepare another bowl with ice and water. Remove the bowl of Zabaglione from the saucepan and place it on the other bowl so that the bowl of Zabaglione touches the icy water. Whisk the mixture continually for another 5–8 minutes or until the sauce cools and thickens – it will still look very fluffy.

Gently fold the chilled whipped cream into the Zabaglione. Pour the mixture into individual serving dishes and place in the freezer for 40 minutes. Serve the iced Zabaglione while it is still easy to spoon.

Serves 4

360 ml/12 fl oz/1½ cups whipping (light whipping) cream

4 egg yolks

4 tbsp caster (superfine) sugar

8 tbsp marsala wine or Grand Marnier

My Secrets
If you wish to prepare this dessert well in advance, you can easily freeze it and, to achieve the correct temperature and consistency, move it from the freezer to the fridge 3 hours before serving.

Use no more than 5 egg yolks at a time when making Zabaglione. If you wish to make a large quantity, do so in several batches.

Semifreddo al Torroncino

Nougat ice cream

Serves 6–8

3 eggs, separated

3 tbsp caster (superfine) sugar

300 g/10 oz/1½ cups mascarpone cheese

100 g/3½ oz/½ cup nougat, chopped

a few coffee beans or crushed hazelnuts, for decoration

Italian homes have lots of nougat to enjoy at Christmas, so this delicious dessert is perfect for the festive season. It can be served with a hot espresso poured on top, which is called Affogato al Caffé, *meaning 'drowned in coffee'. The method for this recipe is very similar to Tirami Su' (Lift me up), on page 141.*

In a mixing bowl, beat the egg yolks with the sugar until pale and fluffy. Add the mascarpone and keep beating, then stir in the chopped nougat.

In a large bowl, whisk the egg whites until firm and fold them into the yolk mixture.

Line a 1 kg/2 lb rectangular cake tin with a large sheet of plastic wrap, pushing it carefully down against the bottom and sides. Pour the mixture into the mould, and freeze for several hours.

To serve, unmould the Semifreddo onto a serving dish and decorate with coffee beans or crushed hazelnuts.

My Secret
Lining the cake tin with plastic wrap will make it easier to unmould the ice-cream when it is ready to serve: the plastic wrap prevents the mixture sticking to the sides of the tin and, once unmoulded, it will peel off easily.

Spuma di Fragole

Strawberry mousse

Other berries, such as raspberries or loganberries, can be used instead of strawberries in this delicious dessert.

Reserve a few berries to use as decoration. Place the remaining berries and the lemon juice in a food processor and process at maximum speed until the fruit is liquidized. Measure out 150 ml/5 fl oz/½-⅔ cup of purée and set aside.

In a large bowl, whisk the egg yolks while gradually adding the sugar. Keep whisking until the mixture is very fluffy and pale. Add the fruit purée and vanilla and keep whisking. Set aside.

Whip the cream until firm but not stiff and place in the fridge.

In a small saucepan, bring 4 tablespoons of water to a boil, then turn the heat off. Sprinkle the gelatine over the surface and stir – the gelatine will look grainy. After 2 minutes, stir again and the liquid will become clear. Stir the gelatine into the strawberry mixture until thoroughly combined. Set aside.

Whisk the egg whites until stiff. Fold the chilled whipped cream into the strawberry mixture, then fold in the egg whites.

Pour the mousse into a glass bowl and refrigerate for 3 hours or until set. Decorate with the reserved fresh berries before serving.

Serves 8

240 g/8 oz/1¼ cups fresh strawberries

juice of ½ lemon

3 large eggs, separated

240 g/8 oz/1 heaping cup caster (superfine) sugar

a few drops of vanilla extract

500 ml/1 pint/2½ cups double (heavy) cream

15 g/½ oz/1 tbsp powdered gelatine

My Secrets

Gelatine requires practice. Do not despair if it looks grainy when sprinkled into the water – just wait and you'll see it dissolving before your eyes. Never reheat the gelatine directly on top of the stove. Vegetarian gelatine is available if you prefer to use it.

A good way to test if the whites are stiff enough is to turn the bowl upside down. The beaten whites will not drop out!

When folding in the egg whites, use a large spatula or spoon and add one-third of the whites at a time, folding them in slowly. Never use a whisk to fold egg whites.

Canditi di Riccione

Fruit skewers

Make as many as you wish

a selection of fruits in season, such as apples, apricots, cherries, grapes, pears, plums and strawberries

½ lemon

vegetable oil, for brushing

3 tbsp caster (superfine) sugar per skewer

On the Adriatic coast, where I spent my childhood summers, the beach is wide and the sand very fine. You can still see men dressed all in white walking back and forth on the beach, carrying a large tray full of Canditi, *which they sell as snacks. It was a treat to have a candito of cherries or strawberries midmorning, after the first swim. But you do not need to go to Riccione to enjoy these nice skewers, which are similar to toffee apples but have less sugar. Choose fruits that have firm, not juicy flesh. If the fruit is too juicy, the sugar will melt, spoiling the final result.*

Wash and dry the fruits and cut them into 2 cm/1 in chunks. Alternate pieces of the fruit on wooden skewers to give an attractive combination of colours.

Lay out a sheet of non-stick paper and brush it with vegetable oil. Place all the skewers on the paper and set aside.

In a small non-stick saucepan, melt the sugar with a little water until the sugar caramelizes and turns the colour of dark rum. Pour the caramel over the fruit skewers. Chill before serving.

My Secrets
Ensure that the fruit is dry, as any juice will melt the sugar, spoiling the final effect.

When dicing apples and pears, make sure that you rub the cut surfaces with half a lemon. The lemon juice prevents the fruit darkening. Then, pour the sugar only on the skin side of the fruit so that it stays nice and crunchy.

The Canditi cannot be prepared too far in advance of serving as the sugar will melt.

Aranci Caramellati al Grand Marnier

Caramelized oranges with Grand Marnier

This is a very simple way to serve oranges at the end of a meal. Its appeal lies in the combination of crunchy sugar and nuts with the fresh taste of the marinated fruit. The result is very refreshing and would go well with a rich chocolate cake.

Using a zester, remove most of the rind from the oranges, making small ribbons as small as a match. Set aside.

Peel the oranges with a sharp knife, discarding all the white pith, then cut them in half. Place in a serving dish and pour the Grand Marnier on top. Add the toasted almonds or pistachios.

To caramelize the sugar, in a small saucepan combine it with a little water, to reach the consistency of wet sand. Turn the heat on and let it cook without stirring until the sugar turns golden and starts smoking.

Add the orange zest to the caramel, stir with a wooden spoon and pour the mixture immediately onto the orange halves. Do not toss. Chill before serving.

Serves 6–8

4 firm, juicy oranges

4 tbsp Grand Marnier

2 tbsp toasted flaked almonds or pistachio nuts

4 tbsp caster (superfine) sugar

My Secrets

Try to make this dessert only an hour before serving as the sugar, when in contact with the orange juice, will melt and lose its crunchy texture.

When adding the orange zest to the caramelized sugar, you will notice that the zest seems to fry in the liquid sugar. At this point be quick about removing the pan from the heat, as the sugar can burn in seconds.

Pesche all'Amaretto e Cioccolato

Chocolate and amaretto peaches

Serves 4

4 well-ripened yellow flesh peaches

8 amaretti biscuits

1 tbsp unsweetened cocoa powder

caster (superfine) sugar, to taste

a little rum

60 g/20 oz/¼–½ cup butter

icing (confectioner's) sugar, sifted, to serve (optional)

Peaches are delicious in Romagna, which in summer is the orchard of Italy. This recipe brings back memories of my childhood, long summer holidays on the Adriatic coast. The pudding is most tempting served with a scoop of vanilla ice cream or whipped cream.

Preheat the oven to 180°C/350°F/Gas 4. Cut the peaches in half and take out the stone. With a teaspoon, gently scrape out some of the pulp so that the cavity in the peach is enlarged to the size of half an egg. Reserve the pulp.

In a bowl, crush the amaretti buscuits with the back of a spoon. Add the peach pulp, cocoa powder and sugar. Stir, adding a little rum to help the ingredients blend – the quantity of rum required depends on how juicy the peach pulp is.

Stuff the peach halves with the amaretti mixture and dot each one with a small knob of butter. Lay the filled peaches in an ovenproof dish with a little water and rum on the bottom, just to prevent them from sticking to the dish.

Bake for about 30 minutes or until you see a little crust forming on the stuffing and the flesh of the peach starts to look wilted. The cooking time depends on how ripe the peaches are.

Serve warm with ice-cream, or cold. When cold, dust with a little icing (confectioner's) sugar just before serving.

My Secret
I can only advise that you make a double quantity of these peaches, because they are so delicious that there is never enough.

Salame di Cioccolato
Chocolate salami

Children love this simple recipe, but since it is so unusual, it can very well be served at the end of a sophisticated supper accompanied by fresh fruit salad.

In a bowl, whisk the butter and sugar together until pale and fluffy. Add the beaten eggs and cocoa powder.

Place the biscuits (plain cookies) in a plastic bag and crush them. Add them to the chocolate mixture along with the chopped almonds and stir until combined.

Shape the mixture into a long sausage, wrapping it in parchment paper. Place in the fridge for at least 3 hours before serving cut into slices.

Serves 8–10

120 g/4 oz/½ cup unsalted butter

120 g/4 oz/½ cup caster (superfine) sugar

2 large eggs, beaten

120 g/4 oz/½ cup unsweetened cocoa powder

210 g/7 oz/1 cup dry sweet biscuits (plain cookies), such as morning coffee biscuits or graham crackers

120 g/4 oz/½ cup toasted almonds, chopped

My Secrets
When crushing the biscuits (plain cookies) in the plastic bag, it is best to use your hands to avoid turning them into fine crumbs. You want small pieces of biscuit, not biscuit powder.

Similarly, chop the toasted almonds with a knife on a board. Do not use a food processor as the almonds will turn to powder.

Chocolate Salami keeps very well in the fridge, if nobody finds it!! It can also be frozen.

Semifreddo alla Panna e Cioccolato

Ice cream cake

Serves 8

300 ml/10 fl oz/1¼ cups whipping (light whipping) cream

2 large eggs, separated

1 lemon zest

60 g/2 oz/1½ cups toasted almonds, or hazelnuts

4 tbsp caster (superfine) sugar

60 g/2 oz/scant ½ cup dark (semi-sweet) chocolate, chopped

No need of an ice cream maker for this recipe that is always welcome to end a dinner party. It is delicious served with raspberry sauce.
The sweetness of the ice cream is balanced by the tartness of the fresh raspberries.

Coat a 1 litre/2 pint mould (Madeira cake shape) with cling film as in the recipe for Semifredo al Torroncino (Nougat Ice Cream) on page 144.

Beat the egg yolks with the sugar until pale and fluffy and doubled in volume.

Grate the lemon zest, making sure that you don't grate the white pith of the lemon skin, which is bitter. Leave aside.

Chop the chocolate: a knife works best; a food processor will turn chocolate into dust. Leave aside.

Chop the nuts and leave aside.

Beat the cream until firm. Reserve in the fridge.

Beat the whites until firm and leave aside.

Now, with all your ingredients ready, you can mix them to make the ice cream.

Add the chocolate, the nuts, the lemon zest to the egg yolks and mix well with a spoon. You'll get a very dense mixture.

Fold the whipped cream and, last, the egg whites gently into the egg yolk mix.

Pour the mixture into the mould lined with cling film. Freeze for at least three hours.

When ready to serve, tip it onto a serving dish and peel off the cling film. Easy!

My Secrets:
This ice cream can be frozen for up to three months. When deep frozen, move it from the freezer to the fridge for about two hours. It will then be perfectly easy to slice.

Terrina di Ricotta e Lamponi

Ricotta pot with raspberries

This recipe is like a cross between a soufflé and a light cheesecake crowned with berries.

Preheat the oven to 200°C/400°F/Gas 6. Grease an ovenproof baking dish with butter.

Separate the eggs then, in a large bowl, beat the whites until stiff. Reserve in the fridge.

In a mixing bowl, beat the egg yolks with the sugar for about 10 minutes, until pale and creamy. While still beating, add the ricotta, cream, lemon zest, and vanilla.

Fold in the pistachio nuts, if using, then the beaten egg whites. Pour the mixture into the greased baking dish. Decorate with the berries and bake for about 20 minutes, or until the tops have nicely browned. Serve immediately.

Serves 6

2 large eggs, separated

5 tbsp caster (superfine) sugar

500 g/1 lb ricotta cheese

3 tbsp single (light) cream

grated zest of 1 lemon

a few drops of vanilla extract

3 tbsp pistachio nuts (optional)

500 g/1 lb/4 cups raspberries or strawberries

My Secret
Make sure that you beat the yolks and sugar until really pale and fluffy. This may take a good 10 minutes but it will guarantee that the mixture is full of air, really light and delicate.

Terrina agli Agrumi
Citrus terrine

Serves 6

2 red (ruby) grapefruit

1 white (yellow) grapefruit

2 navel oranges

2 tangerines

1 tbsp candied fruit strips
(see recipe on page 153)

300 ml/10 fl oz/1¼ cups
sweet white wine, such as
Muscat

100 g/3 oz ½ cup caster
(superfine) sugar

4 tsp powdered gelatine
(unflavoured gelatine)

*This is one of my favourite desserts, as it is light and very refreshing.
The presentation is beautiful and the method quite easy, though it
requires many steps. I suggest that you serve it in winter, when all the
citrus fruits are at their best.*

Using a sharp knife, peel all the fruit. Remove all white pith, as well
as membranes between each segment.

Chop all the candied fruit strips (they can be prepared in advance
and kept chilled).

Arrange the fruit segments and candied fruit attractively in a loaf tin
or similar. (The total capacity of the tin should be about 1 litre/
2 pints.)

In a small saucepan, bring the Muscat and sugar to the boil for about
2 minutes until the sugar is dissolved. Remove the saucepan from
the heat and sprinkle the gelatine into it. Add 200 ml/7 fl oz water to
the saucepan and leave it to cool down slowly, stirring occasionally.

When almost cool but not set, gently pour the mixture on to the fruit.
Chill, covered, overnight, then serve chilled.

My Secret
The best way to unmould any gelatine mould is to dip a thin knife
into hot water, then run it around the edge of the mould. If using a
rounded mould, dip it into a sink full of hot water for a few seconds
and the pudding will come out like magic!

Scorzette Candite

Candied fruit strips

Do not underestimate the moreish appeal of these little strips. Their flavour is very powerful and makes all the difference in the Citrus terrine recipe on page 152. If you prefer, you can use orange or lemon instead of grapefruit.

Using a potato peeler, remove the rind from the grapefruit in large pieces. With a sharp knife, remove any white pith, as it has a bitter taste.

Stack the pieces of rind three or four high, then cut them lengthways into thin strips.

Fill a saucepan with water, then add the strips. Bring to the boil. Simmer for 10 minutes, then drain through a sieve. This will take away some of the bitterness of the rind.

In a small saucepan, mix 150 ml/5 fl oz water, the sugar and the glucose. Bring to the boil, stirring, until the sugar has dissolved.

Add the rind strips and simmer gently over a low heat for 15–20 minutes until the strips are translucent and the syrup has thickened.

Cool the strips in their syrup, then cover and chill. The strips can be kept in the fridge for about two weeks.

Makes varying quantities of fruit strips

1 large grapefruit

60 g/2 oz caster (superfine) sugar

1 tbsp liquid glucose

My Secret

The glucose is crucial to the success of this recipe. I once tried to use golden syrup instead of glucose, and I can assure you that it didn't work!

Budino al Limone

Lemon pudding

Serves 6

1 very large unwaxed lemon

175 g/6 oz/¾ cup caster (superfine) sugar

175 g/6 oz/1½ cups ground almonds

1 tbsp rum, Grand Marnier or limoncello

6 eggs

butter and fresh breadcrumbs for coating the mould

icing (confectioner's) sugar, for dusting

When a friend gave me an antique Italian cookery book on my most recent trip to Italy, I was really intrigued by the method for this recipe. However, it is exquisite and will be a great success at the end of a light spring meal.

Cook the lemon, covered with water, for 2 hours. Pass it through a sieve, then add the sugar, almonds, liqueur and egg yolks. Mix well with a spoon.

Whip the egg whites and gently fold into the lemon mixture.

Coat a 1 litre/2 pint creme caramel-type mould with butter then breadcrumbs to prevent the pudding from sticking to it. Gently pour the lemon mixture into the mould.

Bake in a moderate oven preheated to 180°C/350°F/Gas 4 for 35–40 minutes. Unmould and dust with icing (confectioner's) sugar.

Serve with a tangy sauce, such as raspberry coulis or lemon curd.

My Secret
When using ground nuts, make sure they taste fresh, not stale. If you are not sure of their freshness, toast them in a low oven for a few minutes to refresh them.

Budino al Cioccolato

Chocolate pudding

The recipe for this chocolate pudding is very simple and not sophisticated at all. It was a classic of Italian family cookery, before you could buy ready-made chocolate pudding mix, which often tastes of flour and has a gluey aftertaste. This version, on the other hand, is simply delicious.

For the caramel, put 2 tablespoons of caster sugar in a saucepan, add 1 teaspoon of water and heat until it reaches the colour of dark rum. There is no need to stir it – just swirl the pan to move the sugar around.

Pour the caramel into a mould, turning the mould to coat it well. Bring the milk to the boil and add the chocolate, remaining caster sugar and the savoiardi biscuits.

Cook gently, stirring, for about 30 minutes, making sure that the mixture doesn't stick to the bottom of the pan.

Remove the pan from the heat and pass the mixture through a sieve. Let it cool completely, stirring occasionally to prevent a skin from forming.

In a bowl, mix the eggs and vanilla extract with a fork, until the eggs are well incorporated.

Mix the eggs into the cooled chocolate mixture, then pour into the caramel-coated mould.

Cook in a bain-marie at 180°C/350°F/Gas 4 for 50 minutes to 1 hour. Leave to cool before unmoulding and serve chilled with whipped cream.

Serves 6

80 g/2½ oz/¼ cup caster (superfine) sugar, plus 2 tbsp for the caramel

800 ml/1½ pints/3 cups whole milk

60 g/2 oz/scant ½ cupdark (semi-sweet) chocolate, chopped

6 savoiardi biscuits, crumbled

3 whole eggs

few drops vanilla extract

My Secret
To unmould the pudding easily, run a sharp knife round the inside of the mould before easing it out.

Soufflé Freddo al Cappuccino

Cold cappuccino soufflé

Serves 6–8

3 eggs, separated

200 g/7 oz caster (superfine) sugar

80 ml/3 fl oz/⅓ cup espresso coffee

few drops of vanilla extract

500 ml/1 pint/2 cups whipping (light whipping) cream

1 sachet (envelope) gelatine (unflavoured gelatine)

This really is quite a special pudding. It is so delicious yet extremely easy to prepare. The only thing that requires special attention is the melting of the gelatine.

Using an electric whisk, beat the yolks with the sugar until they are very pale and doubled in volume.

Still beating, add the coffee and vanilla extract. In a separate bowl, whip the cream to soft peaks and reserve.

Prepare the gelatine. Bring 60 ml/2 fl oz water to the boil. Turn the heat off as soon as it starts boiling. Sprinkle the gelatine on to the water and stir to dissolve. Leave to cool.

In the meantime, beat the egg whites to soft peaks.

To assemble all the ingredients: pour the gelatine in a thin thread on to the egg and coffee mixture, while stirring. Fold in the cream and, finally, the egg whites.

Pour into a glass bowl or individual cappuccino cups and chill for at least three hours. Sprinkle with a little cocoa powder before serving.

My Secret

You will notice that gelatine looks very grainy when you first put it in the boiling water. It must dissolve completely before you add it to the eggs. Just stir it with a spoon and wait until completely dissolved. Never boil gelatine.

Use very, very strong coffee. If you do not have an espresso machine, just melt some instant coffee into a very dark coffee. It should be so dark that you wouldn't want to drink it.

Index

Anna Venturi and Venturi's Table
Corporate Cookery Centre

'We don't need to impose teambuilding. It just happens.'

During a Venturi's Table cookery experience, businesspeople create a delicious three-course meal in a welcoming environment and enjoy it together, around the table. Groups can choose to cook from three cuisine types – classic Italian, Indian, or sushi.

Each cookery experience lasts four hours with an emphasis on fun, relaxation and enjoyment. Rather than mindless amounts of chopping or arm-straining mixing, participants are invited to 'sip and stir', enjoying fine wines as they cook. At the end of their session, hungry, fully relaxed teams sit down together and are served the gourmet food they have created. Companies can also add an hour long wine-tasting session to their experience which takes them on a tour of Italy's main wine regions.

Visit: www.venturis-table.com for more information.

'Forget paintballing: companies turn to a new bonding recipe.'
The Guardian
'Culinary classes with the recipe for making a team.'
The Financial Times
'Companies send staff to the kitchen.' *The Daily Telegraph*
'A taste of Blackberry pie.' *The Independent on Sunday*
'Cookery classes are the latest popular pastime for City workers.'
The Evening Standard
'Firms are sending staff for cookery lessons.' *The London Lite*

After over 10 years of teaching people how to cook Italian food, Anna Venturi opened Venturi's Table Corporate Cookery Centre with her daughter Letizia Tufari in 2005. The cookery centre is the first in the UK to offer cookery experiences exclusively for the corporate market. Custom-built by Anna and Letizia in London's Wandsworth Town, Venturi's Table boasts two aspirational kitchens, worth over £150,000 each, which combine stunning Italian high-spec design with powerful technology. Since opening, Anna and Letizia have hosted the likes of Google, Sony, Microsoft, BP, L'Oreal Paris, eBay, Coca-Cola, Selfridges, Barclays and De Beers who have sent their top executives to cook and share delicious food together.

The biggest names in international business do not come to Venturi's Table for cookery instruction. The centre's cookery experiences are all about using the process of cooking and sharing delicious food as a way to develop professional relationships, motivate and encourage under-pressure teams and inspire best performance. For centuries, families have used the kitchen and the dining table as a way to bring people together and help people feel part of something special. Venturi's Table applies these principles to business life.

Venturi's Table is a welcome addition to the teambuilding market. In just three years the centre has helped over 7,000 business professionals bond 'without noticing'.' There are no flip charts, score cards or anything at all which would give businesspeople the impression they are on a corporate 'teambuilding' experience at the centre. Following their time at Venturi's Table, again and again companies experience a real improvement in the way their staff interact. Corporate relationships are genuinely deepened and not just temporarily 'forced' with obviously contrived activities justified with business jargon.